IRELAND DURING THE SECOND WORLD WAR

CAXTON EDITIONS

AN IMPRINT OF CAXTON PUBLISHING GROUP
20 BLOOMSBURY STREET, LONDON WC1 3JH

ISBN 1 84067 418 0

A COPY OF THE CIP DATA IS AVAILABLE FROM THE
BRITISH LIBRARY UPON REQUEST

DESIGNED AND PRODUCED FOR CAXTON EDITIONS
BY POINTING DESIGN CONSULTANCY

REPROGRAPHICS BY GA GRAPHICS

PRINTED BY C.T.P.S.

IRELAND

DURING THE SECOND WORLD WAR

TEXT BY IAN S. WOOD

CAXTON EDITIONS

CONTENTS

ONE ISLAND: TWO STATES

Famously and prophetically, Michael Collins declared in December 1921 that the Anglo-Irish treaty which he had just signed would be his death warrant. For him and his fellow Irish negotiators the critical issue was not the partition of their island, already a reality under the terms of the 1920 Government of Ireland Act, but the nature of the future constitutional relationship between any Irish state and the British Empire.

Britain's objective, over which David Lloyd George and Winston Churchill made it clear they were prepared to resume all-out war, was a settlement based on Dominion status for twenty six Irish counties and continued allegiance to the Crown. Collins and his colleagues signed up to this as a necessary compromise on the longer road to full Irish freedom. The treaty, he argued, offered 'the freedom to achieve freedom.'

Optimists saw it as a basis for ending an ancient quarrel while protecting essential British interests. This, in essence, was Churchill's view. He had come to see the limits to what military force, often brutally used, could achieve in Ireland and he came out strongly for a settlement which would leave the Royal Navy strategic bases in an Irish state within the Empire. To him, this involved no infringement of Irish sovereignty. Sixteen years later his reaction was one of fury and incomprehension when a Dublin government, led by men who had fought Collins over the treaty, saw fit to abrogate the articles which defined the status of the designated ports.

The treaty had to be steered through the Westminster Parliament and reassurance given to Ulster Unionists who feared the Boundary Commission promised to Dublin by Lloyd George would cause their fledgling mini-state unsustainable loss of territory. It was during these debates that Churchill made his gloomy and often-quoted observation about how, after the cataclysm of world war and 'as the deluge subsides and the waters fall short we see the dreary steeples of Fermanagh and Tyrone emerging once again.'

IRA attacks took place along the new border and spread to Belfast, where sectarian carnage reached new depths. In March 1922 Churchill, who had moved

LEFT: General Michael Collins, Commander in Chief of the National Army, June 1922.

from being Secretary of State for War under Lloyd George to Secretary of State for the Colonies, appealed to Collins and Arthur Griffith, President of the Irish Dail, to use their influence along with the Ulster Unionists to bring the killing under control. Collins met Sir James Craig, Northern Ireland's first Prime Minister, and they agreed to an end to IRA operations in the North as well as tougher security measures to protect the Catholic population. Even so, another 150 lives were lost in Belfast alone before the year's end.

Churchill strove in correspondence to convince Collins of the need for the new Free State to co-exist with Ulster Unionists. 'They are your countrymen,' he wrote in April 1921, 'and require from you at least as careful and disciplined handling as you bestow on the extremists who defy you in the South.' He could hardly say otherwise to Collins, for throughout the previous year's treaty negotiations he had held firm for separate treatment for Protestant Ulster.

This was implicit, though perhaps not explicit, in the position his father Lord Randolph Churchill had taken against Home Rule in 1886 and Churchill felt that loyal Ulster, after years of resisting Home Rule, was owed something by his government for accepting the compromise of partition. If this meant military action on the border to support Craig's government Churchill was ready for it, though Lloyd George feared reckless action. This was how he saw Churchill's intervention on 3 June 1922, when he moved 1,000 British troops with artillery into the Pettigo-Belleek area on the County Fermanagh border. This was in response to Free State troop movements on their side of the border and some limited IRA activity. This narrow triangle of disputed territory was just the sort of area that Dublin hoped might be ceded to it if the Boundary Commission set up by the treaty began its adjudications but Churchill's actions inflamed the situation. It was resolved by the withdrawal of Free State forces but Churchill's role did no harm to his relations with the Unionist government.

As this at times melodramatic border crisis ran its course, the Free State and its Provisional Government came under increasing threat from the anti-Treaty IRA. Dail elections in June 1922 gave the pro-Treaty party a clear majority of seats and a real mandate for it to assert its authority against the rebels who had seized the Four Courts building in Dublin. It fell to Collins to order the Free State's new army into action which began with heavy shelling of the Four Courts with British artillery.

RIGHT: Sir James Craig, later Viscount Craigavon, First Prime Minister of Northern Ireland until 1940.

ABOVE: Irish insurrection near Dublin 1867.
LEFT: William Gladstone in the House of Commons, outlining plans for
Irish Home rule 1886.

11

William Gladstone (1809-1898), four times Prime Minister in Queen Victoria's reign, he entered into a political alliance with Parnell, the Irish nationalist leader, and twice attempted legislation for home rule.

Charles Stewart Parnell, (1846-91) and Kitty O'Shea. Ultimately destroyed
politically by his love for Kitty O'Shea, the wife of one of his own party's MPs. But a charismatic
leader and creator of a disciplined Home Rule Party.

These were the opening shots of a civil war surpassing in cruelty the struggle against the Crown forces. It cost Collins his life but the Free State emerged from its first ordeal intact.

Northern Ireland also remained intact despite the sectarian bloodbath amidst which it had been brought to birth and so too did its border. Article 12 of the treaty had set up a Boundary Commission to review the border and Collins left the negotiations under the impression that significant concessions would in due course be made to the Free State.

Churchill denied that he himself had ever led the Irish to believe in such an outcome and by late 1925 the Commission, when it finally reported, ordered no more than a minor two-way transfer of territory to even out the border. William Cosgrave, Taoiseach or Prime Minister of the Free State, responded with a rage born in part from fear for his own survival of the political fallout from the Commission's ruling. He received scant sympathy from the Baldwin government in London and was rebuffed by the Ulster Unionists when he pressed for some concessions on the rights of the Catholic minority in the north if Article 12 was in reality a dead letter.

There was a conciliatory offering to the Free State, though Churchill, Baldwin's Chancellor of the Exchequer in 1925, had his doubts about it. This was British acceptance that the Irish state's repayment of its already agreed share of the National debt be phased over a sixty year period. Irish resentment however remained and could focus on Dublin's continued obligation to make land annuity payments to London as well as to contribute an imposed share of the estimated cost of the post-1918 'troubles'.

This was not the first demonstration of the weakness of Dublin's position. Three years earlier, as the battle raged for the Four Courts, the Ulster Unionists finalised their plans to end proportional representation in local council elections. It was a clear signal to the nationalist community that government policy was to minimise their presence in the administration of local services. Collins was furious but turned for help to Churchill, with whom he had developed an unexpected rapport during the treaty negotiations.

He wrote at some length on 9 August, 1922, urging the need for the Unionists to be overruled and pointing out that the power for London to do this lay in Article 75 of the 1920 Act creating the

Ulster Unionist postcard from before the First World War.

northern state. Churchill's response was a bitter disappointment for he backed off from making the case in Cabinet for what could have become a confrontation of defining importance with the Ulster Unionists.

For a long time, Irish nationalist historians found it hard to see the treaty and partition as anything other than a Machiavellian British strategy to abort the dream of uniting their island's 'four green fields'. In reality, though, there was as tenuous a basis for any workable and non-violent unification of Ireland in 1918 as there was for the continued existence of Yugoslavia after 1990.

Before 1914, Ulster Protestants had taken resistance to their incorporation in any self-governing Irish state to the brink of a rebellion against British authority which was only averted by war in Europe. Neither Unionist nor nationalist communities could see any rationality or morality in each other's case. Nationalists, with a clear majority in Ireland as a whole held to the view, as Dr Conor Cruise O'Brien has put it, 'that they

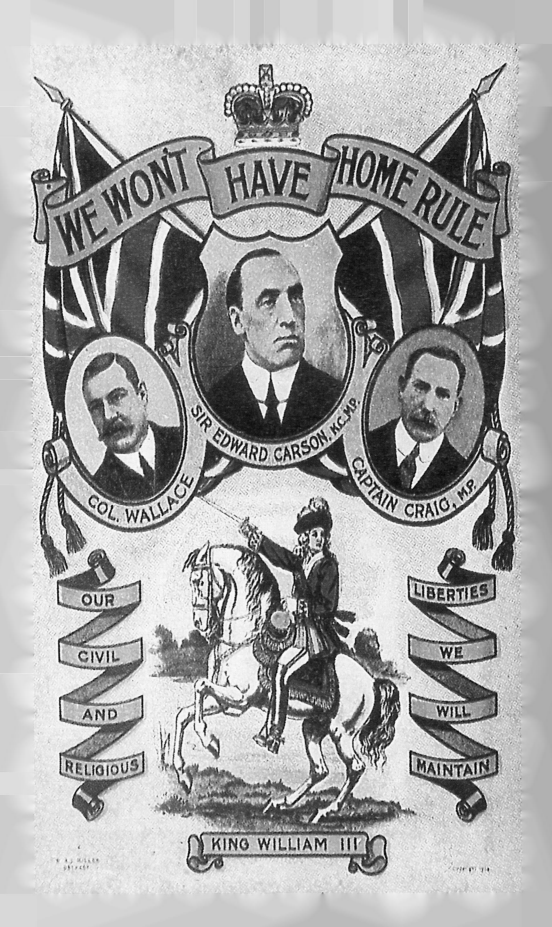

ABOVE AND LEFT: Postcards against home rule .

ABOVE: Ulster Unionists reject the Third Home Rule Bill (1912-1914).
LEFT: Sir Edward Carson, Ulster Unionist leader.

had a right to secede from the United Kingdom but that Unionists did not have the right to secede from the entity they sought to create.'

By 1921, after a surfeit of bloodshed, there was a reluctant will for compromise, to the extent that Unionists like Craig came to accept a partitioned state comprising six Ulster counties as a viable fall-back position, given that they could not maintain the Union in its old form. Republican leaders such as Griffith and Collins, for their part, decided to settle for what was on offer even if a brutal and for Collins, fatal confrontation would result with those who had been comrades in arms until the 1921 treaty.

The 1920-21 settlement did not of course finally resolve the Irish question, but it did re-define it. Most of Ireland won the substance of self-government and as the Second World War showed dramatically, this included the right to decide its own foreign policy even if that was neutrality. After 1945, severing the Irish state's links with Crown and Commonwealth was little more than a formality.

Northern Ireland became a devolved entity within the United Kingdom, its bitter internal divisions masked by the rhetoric of its leaders or converts to its cause like Churchill, who wrote of it in 1933 'We would no more allow hostile hands to be laid on the liberties of the Protestant North than we would allow the Isle of Wight or the castles of Caernarvon or Edinburgh to fall into the hands of the Germans or the French'.

The northern statelet's powers were limited. It had no fiscal autonomy but it did, vitally, control its internal security, subject in theory to reserve powers which remained with the Westminster Parliament. These could have been activated to make a reality of what Lord Carson, charismatic champion of resistance to Home Rule before 1914, came to believe was critical for Northern Ireland in the long term, protection of minority rights. Failure by Unionist governments to do this adequately led the Catholic and nationalist community to develop a strong sense of its victimisation and exclusion from the state.

War, when it came in 1939, provided some ominous proofs of Northern Ireland's continuing divisions. It also threw into clear focus the two Irish states' very different perceptions of their relationship to Britain, and their obligations to it, or lack of them, in the minds of a Dublin government led after 1932 by a hero of both the Easter 1916 rising and of the anti-Treaty cause six years later, Eamon de Valera.

ABOVE: Group photograph in front of Belfast City Hall from the 1920s including, third from the left, JM Andrews who was Prime Minister of Northern Ireland, 1940-43.

ABOVE: Tens of thousands of Southern Irishmen volunteered to join the British Army in the First World War.

LEFT: Unionist Leader, Sir Edward Carson, with Sir James Craig beside him, signs the Ulster Covenant at Belfast City Hall on September 28, 1912, on what became known as Ulster Day. The covenant set out implacable Protestant opposition to Home Rule. Some signed in their own blood.

ABOVE: The first sitting of the Northern Ireland Parliament to elect a speaker at Belfast City Hall on 7 June 1921.

The War of Independence between the IRA and British Army ended with a truce on 11 July 1921.

In the six northern counties, the Unionist Party under Sir James Craig set up the first Northern Ireland government.

ABOVE: Members of the House of Commons, first Parliament of Northern Ireland,
June, 1921. Sir James Craig, Prime Minister until 1940, is on the front row, sixth from the left. J.M.
Andrews, Prime Minister from 1940-1943, is also in the front row, third from the right.
RIGHT: In May 1921 Carson took a peerage and became Lord Carson of Duncairn. He used his seat in
the House of Lords to make bitter attacks on what he saw as the treachery of partition and the 1921
treaty. In May 1923 he visited Belfast and this album was presented to him as tribute from Unionists at
an emotional rally in the Ulster Hall.

ABOVE: David Lloyd George, the British Prime Minister who negotiated with Michael Collins.

ABOVE: Michael Collins with General Mulcahy, August 1922.

ABOVE: De Valera rejecting the treaty between Britain and Ireland and denouncing the provisional government of Ireland.

ABOVE: A mass meeting in Sackville Street (now O'Connell Street) Dublin. De Valera addresses the crowd in support of a resolution declaring that Ireland is not part of the British Empire and renewing allegiance to the republic.

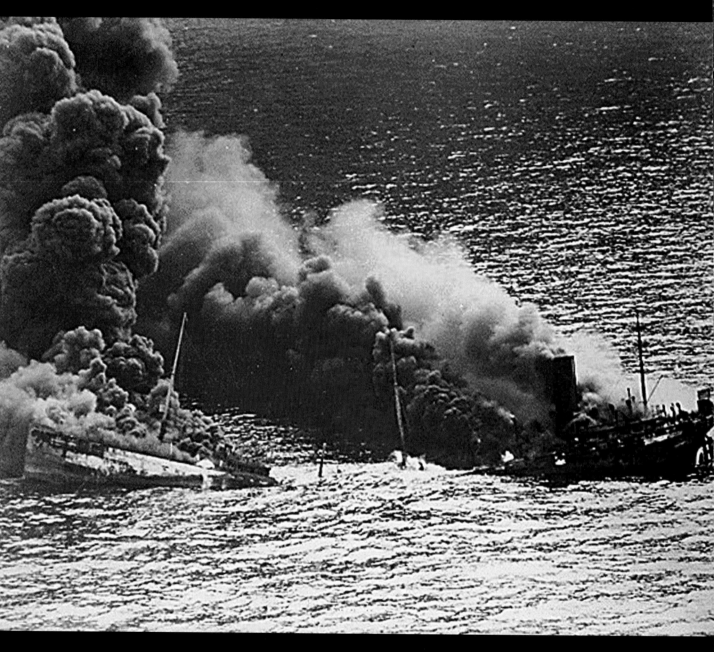

An Allied tanker, torpedoed in the Atlantic Ocean by a German submarine, crumbles amidship under the heat of fire, then sinks. March 1943.

CHAPTER 1

EIRE'S NEUTRALITY

There are several thousand British war graves on Irish soil. In some of them, on lonely headlands from the windswept coast of Donegal to Kerry, lie victims of the battle of the Atlantic, Royal and merchant navy crew members whose ships were sunk by the Germans without the protection Eire's ports might have provided, had its government in Dublin not closed them to Britain's forces. The bitterness this caused lasted decades and Irish neutrality in the war against Hitler's Reich has remained a contentious and divisive subject.

'It is not as representing the sentiments or feelings of our people that the government stands before you with this policy,' Eamon de Valera told the Irish Dail on 2 September 1939 when he declared the state's neutrality in the then imminent European war: 'It stands before you as the guardian of the interests of our people, and it is to guard these interests as best we can that we are proposing to follow the policy.'

His announcement was hardly a dramatic shift in direction for the government he had led since his election victory in 1932. In that year he took office with Fianna Fail, the party he had founded six years earlier. In 1927 de Valera, having only recently played a major part in a brutal civil war over the 1921 Anglo-Irish treaty, gave up his pledge to boycott the Dail. This split the republican movement as anti-Treaty elements within Sinn Fein and the IRA bitterly repudiated their former leader. In power, de Valera sought to present himself as a true keeper of the republican flame, while seeking to neutralise the power of the IRA. He followed a policy of economic nationalism, ending the compensation or 'annuity' payments to Britain agreed under the 1921 treaty. This prompted a damaging trade war in which Britain resorted to sharp tariff increases on goods from Ireland. De Valera took other initiatives, highly charged with symbolism, like abolishing the office of

British Governor General, which was central to any concept of the Irish state's dominion status, and he also ended the oath of allegiance to the British crown.

The worst of these tensions were resolved in negotiations in 1938 between the Chamberlain government and de Valera. The trade war was brought to an end and the so-called 'treaty ports' where a British naval presence had been agreed in 1921, were returned to Irish control. These ports were on Lough Swilly in the north and at Berehaven and Cobh in the south, or Queenstown as the latter had been known prior to the Free State's emergence. Any return of these ports and their facilities to British use in the event of war would always, in de Valera's mind, have compromised the neutrality of the Irish state and he gave out many signals before September 1939 that this would indeed be Eire's policy if and when war came.

One of these signals was in a speech de Valera delivered to the League of Nations assembly at Geneva in July 1936. He had taken a conscientious view of the Irish state's participation in the League, supporting strong economic sanctions the previous year against Fascist Italy over its aggression against Abyssinia. Their failure, and the apparent infirmity of purpose of

Britain and France, where real action was needed to uphold the League's authority, alerted him to what he saw as the need for real independence in Free State foreign policy. 'Peace is dependent upon the will of the great states,' he told the assembly in his speech: 'all the small states can do, if the statesmen of the great states fail in their duty, is resolutely to determine that they will not become the tools of any great power and that they will resist with whatever strength that they may possess every attempt to force them into a war against their will'.

This speech, and others like it, gave a clear indication of how de Valera would define Irish priorities in the event of war and even yet goes a long way to provide a rationale for Eire's neutrality in the years of 'the emergency'. One man who could never accept this, however, was Winston Churchill, both before and during his years as Britain's Prime Minister.

After the end of the war in Europe, he delivered a victory broadcast in which he drew emotional comparisons between the role in the war of Eire and the Unionist-controlled mini-state to the north of it. 'Had it not been for the loyalty and friend-ship of Northern Ireland,' he declared, 'we should have been forced to come to close

RIGHT: Eamon de Valera.

34

Ceremonial horse drawn
artillery exercising in the
Phoenix Park, Dublin
in 1935.

Churchill (ABOVE) implied in a 1945 broadcast to de Valera that without Northern Ireland's support, Britain might have had to re-take the treaty ports.

Chamberlain (ABOVE) wanted proof that access to the ports really was the matter of life and death which Churchill claimed.

The Dunkirk evacuation in 1940.

quarters with Mr de Valera or perish forever from the earth. Owing to the action of the Dublin government, so much at variance with the temper and instinct of thousands of Southern Irishmen who hastened to the battlefields to prove their ancient valour, the approaches which the Southern Irish ports and airfields could so easily have guarded were closed by hostile aircraft and U-boats.'

Churchill was implying in this broadcast that without Northern Ireland's support, Britain might have had to re-take the treaty ports and that these ports really were vital to the Battle of the Atlantic. Naval historians, as well as some biographers of de Valera, have queried this, arguing that shipping routes off Ireland's southern coast would have been extremely costly to defend, given their proximity to German air and U-boat bases in France after its fall in June 1940. After that, they maintain, the only safe route for convoys to Britain was along the coast of Donegal and Northern Ireland itself. This of course has little bearing on the symbolism of de Valera's decision not to compromise Irish neutrality over the ports or on the powerful emotions the whole issue still arouses among Ulster Unionists and Loyalists.

Churchill's fiercely-held belief that the treaty ports should not have been returned to Eire had a close relationship to his larger conviction that Irish neutrality had little basis in legality. This made the de Valera government even more wary than it would have been of British intentions when Churchill joined the Chamberlain government in September 1939 as First Lord of the Admiralty. This meant that the issue of the treaty ports remained uppermost in Churchill's mind but within days of taking office he became preoccupied with the belief that German U-boats were being given sanctuary in Irish waters.

By October he was putting to the Cabinet his view that it 'should take stock of the weapons of coercion' against Eire and that the crown's law officers should report on the legality of the Irish government's refusal either to join the war or to give the Royal Navy access to the treaty ports. Chamberlain however was unconvinced. He was alert to the risks of coercive action against Eire and wanted more proof that access to the ports really was the matter of life and death which Churchill claimed it was.

Churchill's language was less intemperate than that of some of his colleagues in Parliament. One of them, Rear-Admiral Tufton Beamish, declared of the Irish in the winter of 1939: 'What a race, what a tribe of outcasts. They are not worthy to survive.' He went on to call for a British re-occupation of the territory of

Frank Aiken and Eamon de Valera examining concrete huts erected in the bog designed for labourers digging turf, c1944.

Eire. Yet little of what Churchill did say at this time was grounded in any real understanding of what de Valera wanted or of how he was seeking to achieve it.

Both Chamberlain and Baldwin, his immediate predecessor as Prime Minister, took a more flexible, even benign view of de Valera's motives than Churchill ever felt able to do. This owed a good deal to the work done by Malcolm MacDonald as Dominions Secretary between 1936 and 1938. He got on well with the Taoiseach, putting up with his jokes about mean Scotsmen and working hard to interpret for Cabinets in London every nuance to what he said, as well as explaining the difficult political context in which any utterance by him, whether on the treaty ports or partition, had to be made.

MacDonald's opinion was that de Valera was essentially a gradualist on the issue of ending Irish partition. He came to trust him and did his best to communicate that trust to Baldwin and then Chamberlain, with a degree of success. Baldwin described the Irish leader as 'a Mediaeval mystic, but straight as a gun barrel.' By the time of the treaty ports negotiations, both Baldwin and Chamberlain had begun to allow for the importance of de Valera's reiterated assertions since taking office that the real independence of the Free State, or Eire, as it became in 1937, was compatible with

Britain's strategic interests, even in time of war.

Irish soil, de Valera often stressed, would not be permitted to any state to use as a hostile base against Britain and in an interview with the London Evening Standard in October 1938, he talked of the real possibility of an Irish alliance with Britain. However, such talk then and on other occasions, of shared strategic and military interests, was without fail coupled with the need to end partition and the historic injustice which de Valera believed it represented.

Irish assurances of concern for Britain's strategic interests could not of themselves prevent plans being made for actual operations on Eire's territory. Events in the spring of 1940 showed that neutrality gave no immunity to German attack and British military planners had to allow for the possibility of German landings in Ireland. By late May, the Irish External Affairs Department and G2, the Irish army intelligence service, embarked upon direct discussions with British officials about military co-operation in response to such an eventuality.

General Dan McKenna, by then Irish army Chief of Staff, was involved too and was instrumental in insisting that any British military movement into Eire's territory could only be after Irish defence forces had gone into action against a German invasion. A British army signals unit was for a time attached to the Irish army headquarters in Dublin to oversee communications with British forces across the border in Northern Ireland. These were rapidly strengthened in the 'invasion summer' of 1940, though Churchill thought this build-up could put pressure on de Valera to co-operate more actively with Britain.

Lord Craigavon, Northern Ireland's Unionist Prime Minister, also intervened with his own bizarre plan, which was for any necessary invasion of Eire to be led by Scottish and Welsh troops. This, he argued, would reassure the population and he urged too, all troops deployed in such a cross-border operation should have Irish language leaflets to give out, explaining the essentially benign purpose of what they were doing.

Northern Ireland's restless national-ist minority was a cause of real concern to de Valera and his security advisers. Many IRA activists there were strongly pro-German and the possibility of German agents arming them and German airborne forces co-operating with them had to be allowed for. The Reich's Abwehr, or intelligence service, in fact over-estimated the IRA's military potential but alarm bells sounded in Dublin even in 1943 when

documents were captured by state security forces in a house belonging to Stephen Held, an Irish citizen of German descent. He had played host to Herman Goertz, the Abwehr's most important agent in wartime Ireland and had been in possession of material about an IRA rising in the North with German support. This was 'Plan Kathleen' but it was an IRA document, not a German military plan as such and, as in Eire, many of the IRA's active membership had already been interned in Northern Ireland by then, so the danger of such a rising was past, if it had ever existed.

The crisis facing Britain three years earlier in the summer of 1940 had compelled Churchill's government to consider every eventuality where Ireland was concerned and even to reconsider partition of the island. This indeed was what was involved in the dramatic talks between the British government and de Valera in late June and early July 1940. Churchill was not a direct participant, Malcolm MacDonald acting once again as the vital intermediary. Some accounts suggest that MacDonald exceeded his brief in the concessions which were offered to Eire. What is more important is that it was Britain which made them and not de Valera.

Within the space of one week in these talks, Britain moved from a position of rejecting Irish unity in any form to promising a 'solemn undertaking' to work towards it, not even in return for Eire joining the war, but merely if the Royal Navy could be given renewed access to the treaty ports. Historians hostile to Churchill and anxious to represent him as a vainglorious leader whose role was merely to preside over British decline have made little of this. Even so, it was a remarkable retreat, though one which earned only de Valera's rejection of the British offer.

The Irish leader had his reasons for responding as he did. He had no wish to trade off his state's neutrality for the mere promise of an end to partition from a government whose leader he believed, with some justification, was deeply hostile to him. In the summer of 1940 it was possible too for him to treat the offer as no more than academic in its significance after Dunkirk and the fall of France. He had Cabinet colleagues who were sceptical of Britain's prospects in the war, while senior figures in the Catholic church, like Cardinal McRory, Archbishop of Armagh and John McQuaid, the new Archbishop of Dublin, were talking openly of the likelihood of a German victory.

Churchill deeply resented de Valera's response yet he refused to give up, treating it simply as further proof of an Irish perversity which could be overcome. Luckily for relations between the two states,

Britain's representative in Dublin was Sir John Maffey, who had been Governor General of the Sudan and also Permanent Under-Secretary at the Colonial Office. This background might have aroused de Valera's suspicion, but Maffey was a man of culture and courtesy who came to like de Valera and worked hard to understand his position on Irish neutrality.

His approach was in marked contrast to that of David Gray, America's envoy in Dublin. The Irish historian Dermot Keogh had described him as 'a troublemaker of the first order, who failed to understand the complexities of Irish politics throughout his stay in Dublin.' Potential danger lay in his close relationship with Roosevelt, to whose aunt he was married. Gray's reports to the President were much influenced by his close contacts with elements in the Fine Gael opposition party who were opposed to neutrality and he came to believe that Britain should 'play to this Opposition and try to split the country'. This would have been a counterproductive strategy which was never attempted, partly because there were also American intelligence officers in wartime Ireland who gave Washington assessments of the situation there which were as well balanced as Maffey's.

Roosevelt did listen to Gray and this may have helped to shape his very negative

Portrait of de Valera, 14 April 1941.

view of Frank Aiken, de Valera's Minister for the Co-ordination of Defensive Measures, who visited Washington in March and April of 1941. Aiken, a tough South Armagh man who had been IRA Chief of Staff for a time, wanted American arms for his country's defence forces. These, he argued, would help Eire hold off any German landings until British help came. An uninvited British intervention prompted by perceived Irish weakness, he also argued, would be deeply divisive within Eire. His exchanges with Roosevelt were ill-tempered and his mission failed.

Churchill at least had the benefit of far better advice on de Valera's thinking than that which Gray was feeding Roosevelt. Even so, he continued to believe Eire's neutral policy might change. This is clear from now available Cabinet papers, as

Aiken and de Valera seated with
a group of trainee priests and their
instructors in the interior of their
religious house, c.1941.

well as the diaries of colleagues and civil servants and Churchill's extensive published correspondence with Roosevelt. A striking example of this optimism is his famously eccentric telegram to the Taoiseach after the Japanese attack on Pearl Harbour. 'Now is your chance,' it read. 'Now or never. A Nation once again. Am ready to meet you at any time.'

This was vintage Churchill, right down to his borrowing the title of an Irish Home Rule anthem in vogue during his father's political lifetime. Cabinet colleagues pointed out how easily the telegram could be misinterpreted in Dublin and that de Valera might read it as a renewed offer to end partition. It was more likely an invitation by Churchill to join the war as an ally of the American republic, not just the age-old British enemy, but de Valera was not carried away by it. When the telegram was passed on to him by the British minister in Dublin, his response was a typically dry one: 'I concluded that it was Mr Churchill's way of intimating 'now is the chance for taking action which would ultimately lead to the unification of the country.' I indicated to Sir John Maffey that I did not see the thing in that light.'

Soon after the Pearl Harbour attack, de Valera described Irish policy as being unchanged even though the United States was at war on Britain's side. 'We can only be a friendly neutral' he declared in one speech and on his 25 December 1941 broadcast, he reinforced that message with the words, 'God's blessing be on you, friends of Ireland, this Holy Night, and despite this terrible war, God's peace be in your hearts.' Barely a month after that, American troops began to arrive in Northern Ireland without any previous consultation with de Valera's government. These forces were very quickly accorded an integral role in plans for the defence of Eire in the event of a German invasion. The relentless demands on the Reich of its war on the Eastern Front had already however, made this an increasingly unlikely contingency.

De Valera registered a formal protest at the presence of American troops across the border yet six months later General Dan McKenna, his own army's Chief of Staff was lunching in Belfast with Sir Alan Brooke, Chief of Britain's Imperial General Staff. Brooke thought McKenna a 'rough diamond' yet they worked together on matters of cross-border military

RIGHT: A 'Beehive' hut air raid precaution shelter in the Kilbride training area, June 1939.

concern. Tensions continued nonetheless to simmer away as the war imposed new pressures on Eire's relationship with the Western allies. There were demands from Washington, which de Valera resisted, to put an end to any German or Japanese representation in Dublin and serious tension over the way the German legation there was thought to be using its radio transmitter. How this latter issue was dealt with, is covered another chapter.

Preparations for Operation Overlord, the Allies' planned invasion of Normandy in June 1944, intensified concern over military security. On 13 March of that year, Britain suspended all travel between its shores and Eire's ports as well as cross-border traffic until after the invasion. Other restrictions followed, on telephone calls and the exporting of British newspapers. Eire's High Commissioner in London was placed under something akin to house arrest. This clampdown was carried out in full co-operation with Eire's security and intelligence services whose vigilance had already rendered abortive the work of German agents seeking to activate IRA units.

The D-Day landings went ahead but de Valera had been more preoccupied with the fate of Rome, which had fallen to the allied armies just days before. His government made strong representations to the Allies against the bombing of the city for fear of damage to its Christian and Catholic architectural heritage, especially St Peter's and the Vatican. In fact the city was spared major damage less as a result of Eire's efforts than because the Allies had reckoned they could take the city without a major air attack on it. Soon after they did so, the massed pipes and drums of an Irish brigade recruited from both sides of the border were heard on parade in St. Peter's Square.

As the war drew to its end Britain eased off its restrictions on essential supplies to Eire, especially coal and on 19 July 1944, the Dublin government was able to announce a relaxation of its severe controls on the use of electricity. Tensions remained, however, and could resurface, as when after the liberation of Paris on 23 August 1944, Eire, ahead of the Allies, recognised General de Gaulle and his Free French forces as the de facto government of France.

Another issue was the presence in Germany of Irish people who had agreed to work as broadcasters for the Reich. Some continued to do this until near the end of hostilities. Best known amongst them was of course William Joyce, a political zealot active in British Fascist politics before the war. Known to BBC listeners as Lord Haw-Haw, his fate was to be tried and executed under British jurisdiction in January 1946. There were others, part of an ill-assorted and mostly flawed Irish intelligentsia, some of them drawn to the Reich's cause through the threadbare notion of Britain's danger being Ireland's opportunity. Some ended up in wartime Germany through contacts made before 1939 with the significant number of German and Austrian linguists, archaeologists and ethnographic scholars who had infiltrated Irish universities and the national museum service. They nearly all returned home when Britain declared war in 1939 but many of them gravitated to German radio. As early as the first month of the war, Irish army radio monitors picked up Irish language broadcasts from Berlin.

Many of these efforts were simply eccentric invocations of Celtic/Aryan solidarity and extravagant predictions of IRA successes against Britain. Much of the IRA was pro-German at both leadership level and lower, but its military potential was constantly overestimated in these broadcasts, as indeed it was initially by the Abwehr, the Reich's intelligence service.

One broadcaster from wartime Germany to Ireland, who had been in the IRA, was Francis Stuart. He died aged ninety seven in the year 2000 after achieving real distinction as a writer. Three of his novels, published between 1948 and 1950, *Pillar of Cloud*, *Redemption* and *The Flowering Grass*, are based on his own experiences in wartime Germany and in a devastated and desperate postwar Europe. He was of Ulster Protestant stock, though born in Australia, and was educated at Rugby School and Trinity College, Dublin. He married Iseult Gonne, daughter of Maud Gonne who had inspired some of the finest poems of W B Yeats.

He was interned by the Free State for his allegiance to the anti-Treaty IRA but remained in contact with them. With his marriage collapsing he accepted a university teaching post in Berlin in 1939 but also worked for a time as a courier for the IRA. In 1942 he began to broadcast for German radio and did so until 1944. 'Through Irish Eyes' was the name given to his weekly talks in which he urged upon Irish listeners the merits of neutrality. This, he argued, was a policy in keeping with Irish interests and which would further the cause of reunification. He denounced the arrival of American troops in Northern Ireland in 1942 as an act of occupation of Irish territory and urged

Volunteers at Curragh camp.

Volunteers at machine gun
instruction at the Curragh camp,
Co Kildare.

Churchill to lift the death sentences imposed in August of that year upon six Belfast IRA volunteers.

Although he frequently poured scorn on what he saw as the double standards and brutalities of the Allies and praised the heroism of the German Sixth Army at Stalingrad, saying of its annihilation there that 'The Irish would understand what the German people felt,' he was also ready to defy the Reich's radio service. He refused to condemn the Soviet Union and indeed thought of it as a heroic victim of aggression and he would never use anti-Semitic material in his broadcasts. Nevertheless he had co-operated with the Reich and was lucky to escape retribution for refusing to continue his broadcasts after January 1944.

In fact Stuart was a rootless spirit, attracted on his own later admission, to totalitarian ideologies and leaders as a dynamic alternative to a decadent bourgeois order. Like nearly all who worked with him in Berlin, except those who could be charged and tried under British jurisdiction, Stuart escaped any major repercussions for what he had done, though he was interned for a time by the French military authorities in Germany after the war. He returned to Ireland in 1948 and eventually, in 1991, was admitted to membership of Aosdana, a state-sponsored academy of Irish artists and writers.

He survived an attempt to have him expelled because of his wartime role and treated this as a reason to make his peace with offended Jewish opinion in Ireland, declaring near the end of his life in an Irish radio interview: 'I am intensely sorry for the hurt I gave to any people by appearing to support the Nazi regime.' Stuart was not the only Irishman of his generation who had appeared to do this, though whether Eire's neutrality was compromised by what he did is doubtful.

For de Valera, the Irish historian Dr Ronan Fanning has argued: 'neutrality consisted of a finely calculated blend of principle and pragmatism.' The principle which guided him was the full sovereignty of the Irish state, an aspiration which he saw the assertion of neutrality serving; but neutrality was also a pragmatic choice in the sense that his country's still bitter divisions in 1939 left him little option. Yet once committed to it, de Valera showed himself capable of interpreting neutrality in a way

RIGHT: A Rating of the Marine Service. In the years 1939-46 Ireland's maritime defence took five forms: the Marine Service as a small seaborne branch; the Coastwatching Service, a coastal monitoring force; a port control and examination service, which controlled the movement of merchant shipping and the coastal artillery batteries, which guarded the approaches to five of the country's main ports and deep water anchorages.

The Archbishop of Dublin,
Rev Dr John McQuaid
inspecting a guard of honour
drawn from the 5th Infantry
Battalion, Dublin.

ABOVE: The German Embassy in Dublin during the war years was at 58 Northumberland Road, Dublin 4. The building is now a Spanish language institute. When 'Operation Sealion' (the invasion of Britain) was to have started, a flower pot was to have been placed on a window sill, to alert spies and sympathisers to the Nazi cause that the invasion was underway. It was here on 2 May 1945, three days after Hitler's death, that Eamon de Valera came to sign the book of condolences. No sign today exists on the building to indicate its historical significance.

that was literal and pedantic in its formality.

Nowhere was this more obvious than in his disastrous decision to call on Hempel, the German minister in Dublin on 2 May 1945, to offer his condolences for the death of Hitler, who had committed suicide in Berlin two days earlier. De Valera was accompanied by Joseph Walshe, Secretary at the Department of External Affairs, though others in this department had advised him against going.

The Irish state was seen to be according diplomatic courtesy to an utterly evil regime, which was in fact collapsing. There was no threat to Eire which could arise from the visit not being made. In neutral Sweden and Switzerland, similar gestures were not even considered. The only neutral states which did follow protocol to the letter were Fascist Spain and Portugal, whose neutrality had been benign to the German cause in ways that Eire's had never been. At a time when the full horror of the death camps and the Holocaust was being made known by press, radio and newsreel cinema, de Valera gave to the world a signal of what could only be interpreted as his country's moral myopia. Irish diplomats, especially in Britain and the United States, were left with the thankless task of providing explanations for his

action. Their efforts, as they privately confessed, added up to little more than poor excuses.

Ironically, it was an old adversary, Churchill himself, who came to de Valera's rescue ten days later with the victory broadcast already referred to early on in this chapter. Predictably Churchill lavished praise on Northern Ireland for its supportive role in the war but, in an ill-judged passage, he vilified Eire's neutrality and implied that Britain could have ended it by military action had it so wished. Instead, he stated, he and his ministers had 'left the de Valera government to frolic with German and later Japanese representatives to their hearts' content.'

Three days later, de Valera retrieved all the ground he had appeared to lose after Hitler's death in a broadcast that many of his biographers view as a masterpiece. It was low-key and unemotional in its delivery, with even a hint of condescension, when he made allowance for Churchill's remarks being made in a context of celebration and national euphoria.

'Mr Churchill makes it clear,' de Valera declared in a crucial part; of his broadcast 'that, in certain circumstances, he would have violated our neutrality and that he would justify his action by Britain's necessity. It seems strange to me that Mr Churchill does not see that this, if accepted, would mean that Britain's necessity would become a moral code and that when this necessity became sufficiently great, other people's rights were not to count.' Such a code, he argued, had unleashed war on the world and would do again.

Even so, he went on to commend Churchill for not violating Eire's neutrality. 'By resisting temptation in this instance,' he declared, 'Mr Churchill, instead of adding another horrid chapter to the already blood-stained record of relations between England and this country, has advanced the cause of international morality an important step.'

People who had until then thought of their Taoiseach simply as 'the long fellow', a figure of ruthless and Machiavellian cunning and opportunism, warmed to the style and finesse with which he had outfaced one of the Irish state's most implacable critics. There was an immediate political dividend for de Valera. Later that month, the candidate backed by him and his party Fianna Fail had no difficulty in winning election to the presidency.

The 'Emergency' was over but problems remained, not least for German diplomatic staff in Dublin. Gray, the American minister, had demanded the closure of the German legation and Churchill supported him. On 10 May, the legation's keys were handed over to the Americans and its contents, including the book of condolences for Hitler's death, were later sold by auction in Belfast. For Hempel and his staff, bereft of the Reich which had employed them, financial hardship followed. Hempel may even have received some help from de Valera and Maffey but his wife was a talented baker and was able to sell German cakes to shops and to friends. It was not until 1949 that Hempel and his wife finally returned to their homeland.

There were also German internees, air crew who had crashed in Eire and naval personnel. In June 1945, the allies demanded that all internees should be handed over to them. De Valera insisted he would do this only on the basis of firm assurances that they would not be executed or transferred to the Soviet Union's jurisdiction. These terms were accepted by Britain but captured German agents among the internees remained fearful of their possible fate. The most competent of them, Herman Goertz, panicked and took his own life with cyanide in May 1947. He had long since accepted the futility of his mission to wartime Ireland. A swastika flag covered his coffin and he was buried in a Dublin cemetery in his Luftwaffe uniform.

**Taoiseach's Broadcast
to the Nation**

Reprinted from "The Irish Press," Thursday, 17th May, 1945

PRICE ONE PENNY

Cover of de Valera's Broadcast to the Nation, May 1945.

Troops of the the 25 Infantry
Battalion pictured during a rest
while engaged in a route march
in the Munster area in 1942.
(Courtesy the Hanley
Collection, Military Archives)

ABOVE: Eire's Local Defence Security Force (or Home Guard) on duty at a road-block.
LEFT: 3.7 inch gun detachment of AA Battalion deployed in the Ringsend/Sandymount area of Dublin.

An Taoiseach, Eamon de Valera T.D. and Oscar Traynor T.D., Minster for Defence inspecting a Local Security Force ('A' Group) gun position at Howth in 1940. The Garda Siochana were initially responsible for setting up this force – Senior Garda Officers are pictured on the right. the 'artillery piece' is made of wood and used for training purposes.

Members of the 1st and 2nd Divisions of the Defence Forces paraded through Cork City at the conclusion of divisional manoeuvres in August/September 1942. 20,000 members of the Defence forces and Auxiliary Services paraded past the reviewing stand over a three hour period. (Courtesy the Hanley Collection)

Members of the Volunteer Force in training at Portobello Barracks, Dublin in 1939. The Volunteer Force was established in March 1934. Apart from basic military requirements there was a political consideration in its formation. The Fianna Fail Government, who had assumed power in 1932, was anxious that the Army be more representative of the different political persuasions in the country. By September 1939 the Force strength was some 8,000 all ranks and when called out on active service in 1940 provided an essential core of Junior Officers and NCO's to the Defence Forces of the Emergency (1939-46) period.

25th Anniversary of the 1916 Easter Rising. An Taoiseach, Eamon de Valera T.D. and Oscar Traynor T.D. Minister for Defence inspect members of the 26 Infantry Battalion, a volunteer battalion composed exclusively of veterans of the War of Independence. Dublin April 1941.

Still from Pathé News' Ireland: Outpost of Peace. An Irish Soldier salutes.

CHAPTER 2

EIRE AND THE 'EMERGENCY'

'It was in September of '39, the sky was full of lead.
Hitler was heading for Warsaw and Paddy for Holyhead'

These lines were sometimes declaimed by the Dubliners as a prelude to their great song, McAlpine's Fusiliers, a celebration of the Irish workforce in Britain. The point they were making was a humorous one and many Irish people made the opposite journey, to join the British forces or to find work in wartime industry that was vital to Britain's survival.

The coming of war in some obvious ways accentuated the Irish state's economic dependence on Britain and its dominions. It had merchant ships of its own to bring in essential supplies but, to sail at all, they had to receive allocations of British coal at British ports. During the six years of hostilities nearly half of Eire's bread was imported from Canada. David Gray, a strong opponent of Irish neutrality, later put it in stark terms: 'Everything needed to keep Eire alive as a civilised state, which Irish soil did not produce, she got from Britain or the allies.'

Necessarily, given Eire's limited shipping services, much of what Gray identified as being vital to its economy had to be carried to Irish ports on British merchant ships. As the U-boat toll on Royal and Merchant Navy ships grew, this became a contentious issue in Churchill's cabinet. Some ministers pressed for drastic reductions on shipping space being given to cargo earmarked for Eire. Churchill never applied this to Eire in an overt spirit of revenge for Irish neutrality, but the imperative of winning the Battle of the Atlantic made it unavoidable. By 1941, reductions in supplies of petrol, oil, coal and fertilizer began to bite and early that year the Dublin government set up Irish Shipping Lines, a state-backed company which, in its first operational year, bought eight cargo ships and chartered five more.

This did not resolve the crisis of Eire's supplies. All Irish ships, in order to use British ports, had to get full certification. Without this they could be stopped at any time by the Royal Navy or denied bunkering and repair facilities. Once at sea these ships, even with the Irish tri-colour and the word 'Eire' painted on their hulls, could be attacked, and were, whether intentionally or otherwise, by German air-craft and U-boats: 135 Irish seamen lost their lives as a result. Demands from ships' officers and crews to have their vessels armed for self defence were pressed in the Dail in February 1941 by opposition party speakers but the de Valera government never departed from the view that this could compromise Eire's neutrality.

The sea war and Eire's relationship to it aroused bitterness. Nicholas Monsarrat served as a lieutenant with the Royal Navy on convoy escort duties and based a hugely successful novel, The Cruel Sea, on his experiences. He echoed this bitterness when he recalled the feelings of some of his shipmates: 'They saw Ireland safe under the British umbrella, fed by her convoys and protected by her air force, her very neutral-ity guaranteed by the British armed forces: they saw no return for this protection save a condoned sabotage of the Allied war

effort.' This view took little real account of Irish history and was unjust to many acts of bravery by Irish crews who saved British survivors of U-boat sinkings in the Irish Sea and in the Atlantic. It also ignored Irishmen in the Royal Navy like Commander Fogarty Fegen from Tipperary who captained an armed merchant ship, the Jervis Bay in a suicidally heroic attack against the German battleship Admiral Scheer in mid-Atlantic in November 1940. Fegen won a posthumous Victoria Cross for an action which saved almost an entire convoy.

For Irish people at home, the war at sea meant adaptation to worsening shortages. At the worst point in the 'Emergency', the weekly allowance of tea went down to under an ounce for each person while the sugar ration was cut to eight ounces and butter down to six. Bread was rationed in 1942 and restrictions in the supply of other commodities inevitably drove up prices both on the open market and the less official networks of sale and distribution which developed. These were hard years but never as severe as what British people endured in homes and cities that became the front line by late 1940.

Eire's fuel crisis became acute as Britain cut back on shipping space allocated to coal for Irish ports. Trains began to run off timber and straw as a substitute and the

The Importance of POTATOES !

The drastic reduction in the importation of human and animal foodstuffs renders essential a greatly increased production of home-grown food. An increased acreage of Potatoes is particularly important because POTATOES

- ☞ ARE AN IDEAL AND INDISPENSABLE HUMAN FOOD
- ☞ PROVIDE EXCELLENT FEEDING FOR ALL TYPES of FARM STOCK including POULTRY
- ☞ YIELD FAR MORE FOOD PER ACRE THAN ANY OTHER CROP
- ☞ CAN BE SUCCESSFULLY GROWN IN ALL PARTS OF THE COUNTRY

ORDER YOUR SPRAYING MATERIALS EARLY !

PLANT MORE POTATOES

Issued by the Department of Agriculture

K.A.A.

railway system slowed down to the point where in the winter of 1942 the 200 mile journey from Killarney to Dublin took 23 hours. One Dublin train travelling to Athlone along a line which ran parallel for some distance to the Royal Canal was passed twice by a barge. So bad did the transport crisis become that the city of Limerick ran a stagecoach service to Adare complete with horse teams and a post-horn player.

Private motoring virtually stopped by 1943 as petrol supplies threatened to dry up. To relieve the crisis people were encouraged to dig turf and peat. In urban areas, traditional skills in drying them off had to be re-learned. Long strips of peat and turf hung over washing lines in suburban gardens became a familiar sight while Dublin's Vice-Regal Phoenix Park became a storage area for emergency supplies which were sometimes stacked there to a height of thirty feet.

These were difficulties accepted as the price of Eire's neutrality and those who later recalled the period were able to see it in perspective. One Dubliner, writing in an Irish Times supplement in 1985 to mark the fortieth anniversary of the ending of war in Europe, agreed that 'At the time I suppose we thought we were going through hard times. It was only later when we realised what was happening in other parts of Europe – the saturation bombing, the concentration camps, the sheer horror and misery – that we recognised what a comfortable war we had had.' This was an honest view in retrospect. Few pubs ran out of Guinness and the Gaelic Athletic Association was able to maintain most of its fixture lists, with huge crowds attending a succession of All-Ireland finals at Croke Park in Dublin.

What could and did briefly bring home to Eire the reality of total war, was air power. In August 1940, a German aircraft dropped bombs on a creamery in County Wexford, killing three young women workers and injuring others and on 31 May 1941, parts of Dublin were heavily bombed by the Luftwaffe. Thirty four people were killed, 90 injured and 300 houses, mostly in the city's North Strand area, were damaged or destroyed. This was a serious embarrass-ment to the German Reich which had been stepping up its broadcasts to Eire in the hope of activating anti-British feeling there. The bombing was a result of navigational failure and the postwar West German government paid compensation to the Irish state. Dublin was shaken by this attack but it bore little relation to the slaughter which had been unleashed on Belfast by the Germans a few weeks earlier.

For many Eire citizens the war offered escape from a low wage economy to

LEFT: Acting suspiciously: an Eire Defence Force patrol questions a motorist.

better-paid employment in a besieged Britain where even the comprehensive National Service legislation of 1941 did not relieve an acute labour shortage. Since the Irish state was still in law a Dominion within the Commonwealth, it and Britain were part of a Common Travel Area. This survived the introduction of Irish passports in 1924 and allowed free movement between the two islands. It was an arrangement which depended on co-operation on both sides. Professor Elizabeth Meehan, an expert on the subject, has shown that this co-operation extended to British help to the Irish in modifying the Common Travel concept under the terms of its 1935 Aliens Act.

This measure sought to exclude 'suspect elements' from entering the Irish state either from Britain or anywhere else. These were elements, as Professor Meehan puts it, who might have been seen 'as a threat to a homogeneous Irish culture or as insupportable in a poor economy' and they clearly were seen as including Jews in flight from Nazi Germany.

War, when it came, led both states to apply some controls on movement between them, though neither wished to end it. From 1939 people arriving from Britain at specific Irish ports were required to have identification documents and controls were in fact tightened as the war

went on. Conversely, Britain applied a degree of control to Irish entry. After the fall of France, Irish travellers, whether crossing into Northern Ireland or to British ports, had to have valid identification which could be applied for at Garda stations. In reality it was to the benefit of both states not to impede economic migration and a large net outflow of desperately needed Irish labour was the result. Any danger of Irish citizens being conscripted was averted by British assurances that this would not happen to those who could prove that they had arrived to do temporary war work.

For many of these economic migrants, the lure of relatively high wages was offset by long shifts and virtually compulsory overtime as industry answered the Churchill government's call for total mobilisation on the 'factory front'. For young Irish workers from rural areas or small towns there was also the culture shock of a society adapting, at least temporarily, to the demands of multi-culturalism as servicemen of many nationalities arrived. Real or imagined moral dangers, especially to Irish girls living and working in London and other big cities, became a preoccupation of the Catholic church at home as the press began to report sharp increases in divorce and illegitimacy in wartime Britain.

Some of course chose to remain after the war and for many others the

experience widened their horizons. Noel Browne, a young doctor who would become a fiercely controversial figure in Irish politics afterwards, worked in hospitals in the London area in the later part of the war. He warmed to an atmosphere of cheerful egalitarianism in relations amongst doctors and between themselves and nurses as well as patients. He contrasted this to the stuffy sense of hierarchy which he had experienced in his profession at home.

For those who remained in Eire there was also the chance to widen their horizons if they were of military age and chose to serve in the state's defence forces. These were ordered on 1 September to carry out a full mobilisation but the resources available for this posed some urgent questions about Eire's ability to defend itself. Its armed forces, from the conclusion of the Civil War between the new state and the anti-Treaty IRA in 1923, had deliberately been kept small for both financial and political reasons. An event which confirmed the original Free State's caution about expanding its defence forces was the March 1924 army mutiny over the rate at which soldiers, and especially officers, were being discharged from service. Many of these were 'old IRA' men, as opposed to anti-Treaty hardliners, but the crisis had dangerous overtones and the Cosgrave government showed some skill in defusing it.

This episode deterred de Valera, when he took office in 1932, from pressing for any real increase in the defence forces. In a difficult economic period for the Free State, costs were a factor but so too was the suspicion that some elements in the army were sympathetic to O'Duffy's 'Blueshirt' movement which brought some serious violence into Free State politics in the early 1930s. There were only about 6,000 men in the army in 1932, along with a skeletal reserve force but it was able to mount ceremonial parades with some style and performed a colourful Military Tattoo at the Royal Dublin Society grounds in 1935. Its School of Music was well rated and its Director was a German, Fritz Brase, who was also a Nazi. At one point in this period, he sought leave from the Army Chief of Staff to set up a party branch in Dublin but was firmly told that he must choose between the party and army service. He decided on the latter, though remaining a much sought-after participant in the social life of Dublin's German community, many of whom were also Nazis.

Brase however was not responsible for the army's acquisition of the very Germanic-looking helmets which became the subject of much mocking comment from the British press and newsreel film commentaries after the war came. The German pattern helmets were in fact

LEFT: **Defence Forces in County Cork in 1940. The German-style helmet would soon be phased out.**

bought from the British company, Vickers, in 1927, since the Weimar Republic was forbidden by the Versailles Treaty to export helmets. They were withdrawn from use in 1940 and replaced by a British model. In reality, the forbidding associations of the German-style helmets were belied by the actual level of Eire's military preparedness in 1939.

'The country was almost defence-less when the Second World War broke out,' wrote JP Duggan, an Irish military historian, and the evidence supports his claim. In September 1939 the state's defence forces had only four anti-aircraft guns and its Air Corps's operational resources were minimal. As the war continued it acquired a few Hurricane fighters through salvage operations on its own territory or purchase from Britain, but there was never enough fuel or ammunition for them to assume even a limited operational role. The corps relied upon ageing Anson and Gloucester Gladiator fighters which would have stood little chance against the Luftwaffe had there been any thought of using them in response to the accidental bombing of Dublin in May of 1941.

Only a few hundred men served with the Air Corps and quite a number of them put their flying experience to commercial postwar use. Others acquitted themselves well in the skilled tasks of observing and monitoring German air activity off Eire's coastline, as well as any overflying of the national territory. Information gathered from this work, as with the army's intelligence service, was made available on a regular basis to Britain and the United States after it entered the war. Overall, Eire was fortunate to escape sustained air attack. It could not have resisted it effectively and only a skeletal Civil Defence structure was ever in place to handle the civil consequences of such an attack.

The state's Maritime Service, like the Air Corps, was and remained under army control, and its resources were also minimal. When the war started it had just one motor torpedo boat on order from Britain. The order was increased to six and even within Eire's territorial waters, its role had to be a limited one. In various makeshift vessels its crews undertook crude mine-sweeping operations, relying on rifle fire to do the job. The writer and humourist Patrick Campbell commanded what he later described as a malodorous and grease-encrusted tugboat in Dublin Bay. It was the crew's duty to intercept and board foreign ships which, he recalled, was usually done to acquire tea to supplement their very basic rations. Surveillance of German movements at sea was one task the Maritime service did perform with some

RIGHT: Defence Forces guard a section of the Waterford, Limerick and Western Railway Company's line.

success. Its coastal observation stations were efficiently manned and were commended by the British and American forces for the rapidity with which useful data was fed to them. This acted as a counterweight to some of the wilder rumours about German submarines being provisioned and given anchorage in Irish waters.

Army mobilisation in September 1939 quickly outran the resources needed for it and early in December the government ordered that its war establishment be cut back to 29,000 men. This was a blow to morale as was the IRA's Magazine Fort raid the same month. Grandiosely described by some as 'Eire's Pearl Harbour', this brought about the resignation of General Michael Brennan, the army's Chief of Staff. To replace him the government went well down the hierarchy of suitable candidates before appointing and promoting a colonel, Dan McKenna. This extremely competent officer confessed himself shocked at the state of the army when he took over in January 1940, but as the war entered a new and menacing phase, with German invasions of a succession of neutral states in Scandinavia and the West, he was entrusted with a dramatic expansion in the size of his force.

By March 1941, McKenna had 41,000 men under arms. This rate of expansion involved the risk of recruiting men with IRA backgrounds but G2, the army's highly efficient intelligence service, kept a close eye on them. There was just as much risk of such men infiltrating the part-time Local Security Force, or Local Defence Force, as most of it was re-designated in 1941. Ultimately it recruited over 100,000 men who constituted as wide a cross section of the community as the Home Guard in Britain. One of them, who later became Taoiseach, was Garret Fitzgerald. In 1942 he enlisted in Dublin in a signals unit and talked about his service forty years later, to the Irish Times. He recalled some simplistic sex education lectures from an officer and a training exercise in the country during which he caught dysentery and spent much of his time trudging through muddy fields to the latrines. Above all, though, he warmed to the memory of the unique array of Dublin characters he might not otherwise have met without doing his wartime service.

Despite a rapid build-up of the defence forces, pay remained low. In the army, a soldier's weekly wage of less than thirteen shillings a week was eaten into by compulsory deductions for haircuts, laundry and welfare facilities of a very basic nature. With the British forces offering substantially better pay as well as the chance of overseas service and real action, war in 1939 accentuated a pattern which was already set.

LEFT: Irish Defence Forces on the march.

Lt General Dan McKenna, Chief of Staff of the Defence Forces (Jan 1940-Jan 1949), pictured inspecting a guard of Honour in Mullingar, Co Westmeath during 'Step Together' week in 1943, a seven day period of intensive state publicity for the Defence Forces.

Significant numbers of serving solders simply 'took the boat' or crossed the border to enlist. In 1944, at the height of the battle of Anzio, an Eire-born sergeant in the Irish Guards was asked by an English-speaking German prisoner why, as a citizen of a neutral state, he was fighting for Britain. His reply was simple: 'They've fed me for seven years. Now I'm earning my keep.'

He had clearly joined the regiment before the 'Emergency' but from early on in the war, British army depots did what they could to establish whether Irish recruits had in reality deserted from their own state's Defence Forces. G2 was aware of the problem and in 1945 drew up its own estimates of those who had left during the previous five years: 'There are at present almost 5,000 non-commissioned officers and men of the Defence Forces in a state of desertion or absence without leave.' Many of them, it admitted, had been gone for as long as four years and it accepted that 'there is little doubt the majority of them are or have been serving in the British forces or are in civilian employment in Great Britain or Northern Ireland.'

For some, there was family history to live up to, which was the case with Edward Fogarty Fegen, whose father and grandfather had both held senior naval rank. He had joined the navy as a cadet in 1904 and seen action in the First World War.

He was given command of the 'Jervis Bay' in March 1940 at the age forty eight, and as mentioned earlier, saved most of a vital convoy six months later though massively outgunned by the 'Admiral Scheer'. Despite terrible wounds he stayed on his bridge and went down with his ship and 200 of its crew.

His self-sacrificial gallantry became widely known in wartime Britain, as did the feats of the Dubliner Brendan Finucane. There was a military tradition in Finucane's family but his father, who had been taught mathematics by a young Eamon de Valera, joined the republican movement and fought in the 1916 Easter Rising in Dublin. Brendan followed him into accountancy and then to work with him in England, where in 1938 he was accepted for a short service commission in the RAF. He flew Spitfires in the Battle of Britain and his bravery in action was brought to Churchill's personal notice. Before his death in combat he won the Distinguished Flying Cross and the Distinguished Service Order.

There were many more, including the Eire-born pilot who brought his badly shot-up Lancaster bomber back from a night operation over Germany. As he undertook the hazardous task of landing, he was heard over the intercom observing to his crew: 'Well, at least de Valera's kept us out of all this.' The bravery in the air of

House in Dublin accidentally damaged by the Luftwaffe.

Finucane and of Fegen at sea was matched by countless others, who enlisted in famous regiments like the Royal Irish Fusiliers, the Royal Inniskillings and the Royal Ulster Rifles, as well as the Irish Guards who had a tradition of recruitment from the Irish side of the border. They went through some particularly bloody battles and one of their number, Lance Corporal John Patrick Kenneally, won a Victoria Cross for his extraordinary courage in action in Tunisia in April, 1943.

Leslie Baker, not Kenneally, was this hero's real name and he was not Irish at all. He was from Manchester and half-Jewish, the illegitimate son of a local textile manufacturer. He formed a love of the army through a school cadet corps and then the Territorial Army. He began the war in the Royal Artillery but during a spell of detention for overstaying his leave he found himself in the charge of Irish Guardsmen. Baker was so impressed by their turnout and high standards that he applied to join them. This request was refused, so he deserted and joined a road gang of Irish labourers. One of them gave him an identity card and a National Insurance number for a John Patrick Kenneally who had returned to Ireland. He promptly offered himself to the Irish Guards and was accepted, with a minimum of questions asked. In Tunisia and later in the awful attrition of Anzio, his bearing matched the

regiment's highest traditions and he remained loyal to it until his death in September 2000.

As the war dragged on the possibility of Eire providing more recruits to the British cause than Northern Ireland became a matter of obsessive concern to Ulster Unionist politicians. The Stormont government asked all the service departments in London to go through their records to quantify the national origins of those serving. It was a futile exercise because Irish citizens who went to Northern Ireland to join up could easily be incorporated within statistics of enlistment in the province, while Irishmen in Britain could enlist from addresses there or be conscripted if resident there in 1939. Ultimately, the Dominions Office in London came up with a figure of 32,000 men 'born in Eire' serving in the army alone, while it estimated that 38,000 from Northern Ireland, where there was no conscription, volunteered for all three services.

It was a sterile controversy, unworthy of those who volunteered from both sides of the border. It was also unfair to Northern Ireland with its smaller population than Eire's, yet the issue refused to go away and continued to be argued over in the period of Northern Ireland's troubles after 1969. Politicians in what became the Irish Republic could be as mean-spirited as some Ulster Unionists and in 1983, Fianna

Fail, then in opposition, bitterly attacked the Irish army being represented at a Remembrance Day ceremony in Dublin. They were still in a state of denial over the real history of the years of 'Emergency' and the extent to which many Irish people had felt real guilt over neutrality.

They were forgetting too the real fears in 1940 of a German invasion. The increased likelihood of this as part of a larger strategy for attacking Britain itself led to actual talks with Churchill's government on military co-operation in the event of such an invasion of Eire. McKenna, the Irish Army Chief of Staff, took the realistic view that only British help could defeat German landings in his country but insisted that any British movement into Eire could only come after his forces had first engaged the intruders. The Germans did indeed develop tentative plans for operations in Ireland, though these were based on greatly exaggerated estimates of the IRA's military potential. They no more materialised than Churchill's talk earlier in the war of re-taking the treaty ports. Even so, Irish military planning for a full year after the fall of France in 1940 continued to assume the possibility of a British invasion long after London had abandoned any thought of it.

The Irish Defence Forces could not have coped unaided with either eventuality. Some of the Fine Gael opposition leaders recognised this and one of them, James Dillon, pressed the case for ending neutrality and giving support to Britain. De Valera briefed them privately in July 1940, admitting that neutrality offered no foolproof guarantees against invasion but defending it as the best available option for Eire. He was never as convinced as some of his Cabinet colleagues were of Britain's imminent defeat and threw his support behind the state's security services, especially the Army's G2 unit, in its measures against German espionage and attempts to activate the IRA on their side.

There is good reason to see this as one battle which Eire's forces won. In this they were much helped by the sheer ineptitude of the German Abwehr where Ireland was concerned, despite the Reich's retention of diplomatic representation in Dublin and the listening post it provided. Hempel was often reduced to incomprehension and despair at the crass quality of German intelligence and the incompetence of agents whose movements were easily monitored by the Garda and by G2. Even Herman Goertz, the most experienced German agent, who remained at large for eighteen months, was under surveillance for much of that time, and his contacts were recorded by security officers. His mission achieved little and he soon lost any belief he once had in the IRA's ability to operate with any effect on Germany's behalf.

Hempel arguably did more useful

Dr Eduard Hempel, German Ambassador in Dublin

work for his masters in Berlin by using the Dublin legation's radio transmitter to send weather reports which could assist German air raids on Britain as well as naval movements. These transmissions were widely believed at the time to have facilitated the escape through the Channel and into the North Sea in February 1942 of the battleships Scharnhorst, Gneisenau and Prince Eugen. Naval historians now doubt this but Churchill, in a memorandum to his deputy, Attlee, described it as 'an abominable state of things. Their conduct (i.e. Eire's) will never be forgiven by the British nation unless it is amended.' Hempel's behaviour in fact was never as impeccable as de Valera wanted to believe at that time, or indeed described it as being in the formal tribute he paid him at the war's end.

With the danger of tension becoming public the Irish External Affairs Department put strong pressure on Hempel and he gave them assurances that the transmitter would not be used again. This did not fully satisfy the British intelligence services, especially as Operation Overlord, the planned 1944 invasion of Europe, drew closer. Their decrypting operations revealed renewed pressure from Berlin for the Dublin transmitter to be used and in December 1943, Hempel was obliged to hand it over to representatives of the External Affairs Department and G2.

All this brought Dublin ministers, civil servants and intelligence officers into urgent contact with the dramatic imperatives of a global conflict yet state censorship effectively isolated Irish people from real information about it. This went much further than in other neutral states like Sweden and Switzerland, who had their own correspondents covering the war and providing independent reports and interpretations of events. This was not the case in Eire, which depended for news entirely upon the combatant states themselves but it was news which was comprehensively censored form the very start of the 'Emergency'.

'The strict censorship regime in Ireland kept many members of the public in a state of near ignorance about what was going on in continental Europe.' This was the verdict of Irish historian Dermot Keogh. He was merely describing what in truth was the intention of state policy. What was 'going on in continental Europe' of course, included the Holocaust against the continent's Jewish population, yet this went unreported. Frank Aiken, Minister for the Co-ordination of Defensive Measures, who had responsibility for censorship, was of the opinion that Eire's neutrality precluded the war being presented to Irish people in any kind of moral context, whether through press, radio or cinema.

Aiken, like de Valera, knew of the awful scale of Nazi genocide. Reports of it reached his office in ever-growing volume yet censorship remained rigorous. Even statements about the slaughter by Roosevelt and Anthony Eden, Churchill's Foreign Secretary, were edited to the point where they read as little more than very general condemnations of cruelty which was never given any specific location or perpetrator. At all costs, in the censors' view, Eire citizens had to be insulated from the temptation to make moral judgments which might in some way compromise their state's neutrality.

One central purpose of censorship was to protect basic state security but it was carried to often bizarre lengths. Countless feature films made in wartime Britain and the United States were denied to Irish cinema audiences while books, magazines and newspapers were relentlessly vetted for copy which might be damaging to state policy. Even L'Osservatore Romano, the Vatican newspaper, met this fate over articles it carried in 1941. Given the growing moral puritanism of the pre-war Irish state, film distributors, publishers and booksellers were no strangers to censorship but the 'Emergency' years saw an expanding bureaucracy working tenaciously to cocoon Irish people from the unsettling realities of a world at war.

Elizabeth Bowen, the English novelist who lived through the height of the London blitz, later moved to Dublin and sent numerous dispatches to the British Ministry of Information. Many of these described an atmosphere she found unreal and stultifying, suffused with what she called a lethargic and dreary escapism among the middle class Dubliners with whom she mixed. However, for those who felt the need to break free, there was the chance of war work in Britain or service in its armed forces. Censorship easily reduced the latter group to non-persons. Even their deaths in action and their many awards for bravery were edited out of the pages of their country's press. Family death notices which alluded in any way to their war service were also censored by Aiken's department in case doubt might be implanted in readers' minds about neutrality as a policy.

The late Professor F S L Lyons, in his fine book 'Ireland Since the Famine', wrote memorably of the effects of censorship and neutrality more generally: 'It was as if an entire people had been condemned to live in Plato's cave, backs to the fire of life and deriving their only knowledge of what went on outside from the flickering shadows thrown on the wall before their eyes by the men and women who passed to and fro behind them.' For many, escape from the cave took them to hospital and factory work in wartime Britain as well as to the bloody battlefields of Anzio, Monte Cassino and

A wartime Fianna Fail election poster.

the Normandy beaches. Recognition in Eire, or the Irish Republic as it became in 1949, of the integrity of their choice was long in coming. It certainly was not apparent when the war in Europe finished in May 1945.

In contrast to the joyous scenes in many European capitals, Dublin's response to Nazi Germany's final defeat was a low key one. Perhaps de Valera had set the tone for it by the careful formality of his condolences to the German legation after Hitler's death on 30 April. The Irish Times, no friend of the ruling Fianna Fail party, laid out a page of photographs in the shape of a 'V' but their use of this British victory symbol slipped past the censors. At Trinity College, with its Anglo-Irish and Unionist tradition, some undergraduates flew flags of the victor nations from the roof of the building and provocatively flung a burning Irish tricolour down into the street below. Two students from University College answered this affront by burning a Union Jack in College Green. One of them was Charles Haughey, who would later play a tempestuous role as Fianna Fail Taoiseach and party leader.

ABOVE: Fianna Fail wartime election rally.
OVERLEAF: Still from Pathé News' Ireland: Outpost of Peace.

ABOVE: German troops marching in Poland in 1939. The German 'coal shuttle' style of helmet had been used by the German army since the First World War.

LEFT AND FOLLOWING PAGES: Stills from Pathé News' Ireland: Outpost of Peace. Irish troops on manoeuvres. The Free State's choice of helmet, known as the 'Vickers', was first introduced in 1927. It was based on the German World War 1 pattern, but because of the Versailles treaty, Germany was unable to export steel military helmets. The government commissioned Vickers Ltd of London to supply 5,000 helmets which the company did, using German machinery. They were painted dark green and were used until 1940, when they were replaced by British Mark II model.

LEFT: Still from Pathé News' Ireland: Outpost of Peace.

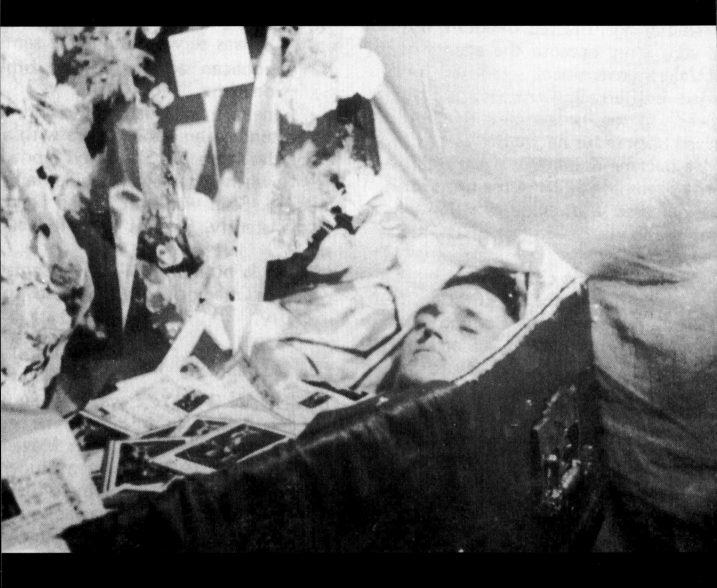

Seamus Burns
Born in Belfast in 1921, he died of wounds after a gun battle with the RUC in Belfast
in February 1944.

CHAPTER 3

THE IRA

In September 1939 the IRA was already at war. As they saw it, they had resumed a historic struggle against Britain abandoned in 1921 by leaders who had signed a treaty which accepted an Irish Free State with Dominion status and an oath of allegiance to the Crown, as well as the partition of the island. Their enemies were not just Britain and pro-treaty republicans but men like Eamon de Valera, who had initially opposed the treaty before coming to terms with the state's institutions, leading his Fianna Fail party into the Dail in 1927 and taking office as Taoiseach or Prime Minister in 1932, a position he retained until 1948.

On 12 January 1939, the IRA's Army Council had issued an ultimatum to the governments of both London and Northern Ireland, demanding an end to partition and the withdrawal of all British forces from Irish soil. There was no response from London or Belfast and four days later the IRA announced its declaration of war. A bombing campaign began in England soon afterwards. The IRA's declared aim was to destroy property without taking life but the use of explosive devices in railway station left luggage offices and letter boxes made this hard to achieve: one man was killed at King's Cross station and five more were badly injured at Victoria.

Worse was to follow in Coventry on 25 August. A bomb left in a busy shopping centre killed five people and seventy others were injured, some severely, from flying glass and metal. The city was to experience infinitely worse carnage two years later but, in a country not yet at war, the atrocity caused a deep wave of anger and revulsion. Two IRA men, Peter Barnes and James MacCormack, were hanged in February 1940 for their part in the explosion but a third suspect was never caught. The bomb had been intended for use against a power station and may have been abandoned in panic. Within Irish republican circles it has always been claimed that Barnes and MacCormack were wrongly convicted.

In fact, MacCormack had assembled the Coventry bomb and Barnes had smuggled it into the city but their plea that it had exploded in the wrong place was never going to save them. Both de Valera and his old political opponent William Cosgrave, leader of the Fine Gael party, made a strong case for clemency to Sir John Maffey, the British representative in Dublin and the British Cabinet took the issue seriously. Nonetheless, the hangings went ahead in face of republican-organised vigils and protests in many parts of Ireland.

The Coventry explosion was the culmination of the bombing campaign which lost momentum as police surveillance intensified. One sixteen year old IRA volunteer, Brendan Behan, was arrested in Liverpool in possession of a suitcase containing gelignite and detonators. When tried there in February 1940, Behan refused to recognise the court and made a defiant speech from the dock. His sentence, because of his age, was only three years, to be served in a young offenders' institution or Borstal, as it was then called. Behan later converted his experiences into a literary classic called *Borstal Boy*. By the time of its publication in 1958 he had radically re-examined the beliefs that took him to England as a teenage bomb carrier twenty years earlier.

In Ireland itself IRA operations continued, though restricted in scope by tough new legislation rushed through the Dail. The Offences Against the State Bill had become law in June 1939 and it allowed the Dublin government to reintroduce military tribunals for cases involving republicans as well as internment without trial. An internment camp was opened at the Curragh in county Kildare and large numbers of IRA suspects were imprisoned there early in 1940 in response to one of the movement's most daring operations since the War of Independence. This was the Magazine Fort Raid. The fort, in Dublin's Phoenix Park, held most of the Irish army's ammunition but just before Christmas 1939 an IRA unit entered it and made off with over a million rifle and machine-gun rounds. Most of this was recaptured by state forces within a week and the wave of arrests which followed gravely weakened the IRA.

Whether the IRA was really as strong as bombing operations in England and attacks in Eire suggested is another matter. Seven years earlier one of the first acts of the de Valera government had been to release IRA prisoners. These were hard-line anti-treaty men who, unlike de Valera, had refused to compromise with the new

Teenage IRA offender Brendan Behan who later converted his experiences into a
literary classic called 'Borstal Boy'.

ABOVE: General Eoin O'Duffy at a rally of Blue Shirts, c1935. To his left is Alfred Byrne, the Lord Mayor of Dublin.

Free State. Their release, along with the abolition of military tribunals for the trial of such men was a calculated risk for the Taoiseach to take, but IRA violence after 1932 was initially directed away from him and the Free State's institutions to vicious confrontations with General Eoin O'Duffy's Army Comrades Association or the Blue Shirts, as they were also known. This was a paramilitary movement of authoritarian views and sympathetic to Mussolini's regime in Italy but its founder had supported the 1921 treaty and taken ministerial office under the Free State.

The IRA still had weapons and was prepared to use them against O'Duffy and in support of tenants in land disputes. In March 1936, some of their gunmen shot dead the retired Admiral Somerville in County Cork because he was known to give advice and references to local men who wanted to join the Royal Navy. This killing prompted a wave of anger at IRA lawlessness and de Valera had it declared an illegal organisation. By this time the IRA was divided politically. In 1934, Socialists within it who thought the movement should take a clear position on class issues broke away to form their own Republican Congress. Many of them went to Spain and fought bravely for the young Spanish republic against General Franco's army insurgents and their Falangist allies.

These divisions and the suspicions they fuelled had not vanished when the Army Council launched its bombing campaign in England. The Chamberlain government's declaration of war on Germany on 3 September 1939 played into the hands of an element within the movement who not only saw the war as 'Ireland's opportunity' but who had active sympathy with Hitler's regime. This was certainly so in Belfast. Paddy Devlin, a native of the city and, until his death in 1999, active in trade unionism and Socialist politics, joined the IRA there in 1940 only to find it urging people to boycott air raid precautions and reporting on British installations and troop movements back to Belfast 'brigade staff'.

By then the IRA leadership was already in direct contact with Berlin. Its Chief of Staff, Sean Russell, was in the United States when the war in Europe started, seeking funds and support from the Irish immigrant community. The American authorities had arrested and held him during a state visit to Canada by King George VI and Queen Elizabeth, but he was later released. With his visa due to expire, he faced the prospect of deportation and the Curragh internment camp so he made contact with German circles in New York. They in turn approached Admiral Canaris, head of the German Abwehr, or intelligence service, who arranged for Russell to be smuggled to Genoa and from there to Germany.

Russell reached Berlin in May 1940, his safe arrival masterminded by Edmund Veesenmayer, a German Foreign Office official whose special responsibility was co-ordinating and supporting subversion in enemy or non-aligned states. Russell began training for a secret mission to Ireland. German sources never specified the precise nature of this mission, though it may well have been to step up IRA attacks across the border in Northern Ireland or even to bring down de Valera and install a pro-Nazi government in Dublin. Another IRA man who came to believe that was Germany's aim was Frank Ryan, who was reunited with Russell in Berlin in July 1940.

Ryan was on the left of the republican movement and fought in Spain as a volunteer for the republican government there. He was taken prisoner by Franco's forces but German Foreign Office intervention secured his release from grim captivity in Burgos prison and a safe passage to Germany. There had been an international campaign to secure Ryan's release but the way in which this was brought about has prompted many questions. Ryan was glad of his freedom and for a time enjoyed the distinguished status accorded him in wartime Germany. Politically, with his links to the 1934 Republican Congress, he was well to the left of Russell and this has raised questions about Ryan's willingness to sail with him for Ireland in August 1940 on a German U-boat.

They never reached their destination and Ryan never saw Ireland again. Soon after the U-boat's departure, Russell developed agonising stomach pains and died on board. British M15 files recently released to the Public Record Office reveal that German intelligence officers in the Abwehr's sabotage section told British interrogators after the war that they believed Ryan had poisoned Russell because of personal and political antagonisms between them. No real proof of such allegations has ever emerged, although Irish citizens living in wartime Germany who knew Ryan, such as the writer and broadcaster Francis Stuart, never thought he had abandoned his anti-Fascist views. However, he seems to have continued to believe that a German victory or a compromise peace with the Allies could bring down de Valera and expedite Irish unification. He may simply have been a courageous but politically confused man rather than part of the hard core pro-Nazi element within the IRA.

Whether Russell's mission to Ireland would have accomplished anything of military significance must remain open to doubt. After the Nazis came to power in 1933 they invested some effort in using the influence they had in the Irish state to cultivate contacts with the IRA. This influence owed much to the Dublin government's readiness to look beyond its own borders and beyond Britain for appointments to major positions. In 1934, de Valera approved the appointment of Adolf Mahr, an Austrian archaeologist and active Nazi, as director of the Irish National Museum. Mahr became head of the Nazis' Auslandsorganisation (foreign department) in Ireland and certainly did make IRA contacts. He is known to have allowed an IRA man 'on the run' in 1937, to hide out in the National Museum's premises, no distance from the offices of the Taoiseach who had only recently proscribed the IRA.

In February 1939, as the IRA began its bombing campaign in England, Mahr would definitely have known of the arrival in Eire of Oskar Pfaus, a German agent posing as a writer, to seek contacts with the IRA. His mission achieved little, partly because he had been badly briefed and made his first approach to Eoin O'Duffy, the IRA's bitter enemy. He did manage to make some contacts and these helped prepare the ground for German Foreign Office backing the following year for Russell and Ryan. All his movements however took place under the efficient surveillance of G2, the Irish army's intelligence unit, which made its findings available to their British counterparts. As for the IRA, it failed to set up the supply routes for German arms which Pfaus recommended and ignored his advice to halt operations against the Irish state in order to give priority to attacks on British bases in Northern Ireland.

Mahr, like the German expatriate community as a whole, returned home when war was declared. This was largely due to the fear that there might be a British invasion to secure the whole of Ireland for strategic reasons. He took employment in the German Foreign Office and his assessments of the situation in Ireland and the military potential of the IRA played some part in such support as there was for the abortive Russell and Ryan mission in 1940. Whatever faith he had in the IRA's abilities was not shared by Eduard Hempel, who

Terence Perry
Died in Parkhurst prison in July 1942, having
being sentenced to 6 years for IRA activity.

Gerald O'Callaghan
Born 1923, he died in an ambush by the
RUC in 1942.

became German Ambassador to Eire in 1937 and remained in office until the end of the war.

This career diplomat was never a Nazi party member but was a willing enough servant of his Fuhrer after 1933. He was always sceptical of the value of German support for the IRA and indeed of the organisation's military capabilities. Overt German support for it, he also felt, might compromise Eire's neutrality and tempt Britain to act, while pro-German feeling could be alienated as well. His judgment was in fact confirmed by events, though the IRA did not lose their capacity to bomb and kill. This simply produced tighter surveillance and a tougher response from the state. In early 1940, two IRA prisoners on hunger strike in Dublin were allowed to starve to death, and in August, after the sentencing to death of Patrick McGrath for his part in a gun fight which killed two detectives, the law was altered to take away the right of appeal against the verdicts of military tribunals.

Operations like the one McGrath had been involved in were pinpricks in terms of state security and Hempel's cynical view of the IRA's ability to destabilise the state or be of tangible help to the Reich was shared by the most important German

ABOVE: Sean McCaughey, born in 1916, was caught by Special Branch men in Dublin. Originally sentenced to death by the Eire authorities for IRA activities, his sentence was commuted to penal servitude. He went on hunger strike and died after four and half years. After his funeral procession down O'Connell Street in Dublin (TOP), he was buried in Belfast.

ABOVE: Sean Martin was killed whilst delivering grenades in April 1940.

agent to be infiltrated into Eire during the war. This was the Abwehr Captain Herman Goertz, who parachuted into County Meath in May 1940. He stayed at large for over eighteen months, far longer than most other agents, before capture, but did not accomplish very much. As stated in a previous chapter, Goertz took his own life in prison in Dublin in 1947, while awaiting return to Germany and certain interrogation. Two years later, the Irish Times published posthumous articles by him which were extremely unflattering about the IRA's organisational and military skills.

After 1941 the IRA was no more than a minor threat to the Irish state but surveillance of its activists was maintained at a high level not just by the Irish authorities but also by the British Embassy in Dublin. One of its more improbable operatives was the much-loved poet John Betjeman, who worked there as a press officer in the early years of the war. Behind a tweedy and bumbling exterior, Betjeman was in fact a competent intelligence officer, part of whose brief was to monitor IRA activity. He decided in 1941 that the IRA, while still dangerous, were becoming more anti-de Valera than anti-British and that a shift in British policy to end the partition of Ireland could bring Eire into the war as an ally.

This did not stop the IRA identifying Betjeman as a threat and Diarmid Brennan, its Army Council head of civilian intelligence, had him followed and considered giving an order for him to be shot. However, after reading some of Betjeman's published poetry, Brennan called off the surveillance. Many years later, when Betjeman had become the Poet Laureate, he received a letter from Brennan, who wrote that 'I came to the conclusion that a man who could give such pleasure with his pen couldn't be much of a secret agent. I may well have been wrong.'

He was indeed wrong. Betjeman loved Ireland and took to introducing himself at parties as Sean O'Betjeman. In 1944, he was instrumental in persuading Laurence Olivier to shoot his patriotic epic Henry V in Eire with a cast of Irish extras, mostly farmers, who were paid more if they brought their own horses to the location. Substantial money was injected into the local economy and the British cause gained in goodwill, but Betjeman's real work continued. Later in the war he was able to brief his superiors on the morale and political leanings of IRA prisoners in the Curragh internment camp, information which was important for assessing their role if and when they were released.

ABOVE: John Betjeman.

Doubts within the IRA itself about the military results it was achieving reduced it to near chaos in 1941. One faction, strongly supported from units across the border in Northern Ireland, claimed that the Chief of Staff, Sean Russell's successor Stephen Hayes, was a state informer. Between June and September he was court-martialled and sentenced to death under IRA standing orders. In reality his confession was beaten out of him but it served to satisfy many IRA members who wanted an easy explanation for military failure. When Hayes made a dramatic escape from IRA custody and sought the protection of the despised Garda, the organisation's credibility, even among those sympathetic to it, plummeted. Hayes was not a traitor to the orgainsation and was later convicted for IRA offences, but the whole extraordinary and brutal episode consumed republican energies for many months.

Ultimately, 2,000 actual or suspected IRA men were interned in Eire during the 'Emergency.' Their incarceration was a key factor in limiting the organisation's ability to operate on a significant scale, though it continued with sporadic attacks. These could still be lethal as in September 1942 when a well-planned killing of a Garda Special branch sergeant, Denis O'Brien, took place in Dublin. This was the first calculated killing of a member of the police in ten years, though others had died in exchanges of fire with IRA units. An IRA man, Charlie Kerins, was later hanged for the death of O'Brien.

British fears had always been that even if the IRA failed to provide a real threat to Eire, they could win support for major operations amongst the nationalist minority community in Northern Ireland,. Then, as more recently, differences within the movement on the two sides of the border were important and the IRA in the North was slower to act than had been anticipated. The nature and impact of its operations there will be considered in a separate chapter of this book, on the war years in Northern Ireland.

By the time the war in Europe ended, the IRA's operational capacity in Eire was at a very low level and much of its membership was demoralised. There was dissension too among the internees at the Curragh. Political fault lines emerged over the bigger issues posed by the war. Some activists on the Irish political left, including a few Communists, were interned in the Curragh and there was an element among the republican internees who were ready to give them a hearing.

A key figure was Niall Gould, a Marxist who had been active in some major Dublin strikes and made links with the 1934 Republican Congress. He ran Russian language classes in the Curragh as well as a political discussion group. Gould encouraged wide-ranging debates, challenging many republican assumptions as well as Catholic teaching on social issues. Senior IRA men in the camp became increasingly concerned and smuggled out a message to the Catholic Bishop of Kildare and Leitrim, in whose diocese the Curragh was, warning him that the faith and morals of internees were being undermined by Communist agitators. Within days, Gould was transferred to Mountjoy prison in Dublin.

Despite diversions like these, conditions for internees were spartan and dreary, but as a strategy to limit the IRA's effectiveness, internment worked, partly because, in contrast to 1971, it was applied simultaneously on both sides of the border. There were of course keepers of the republican flame who resorted to the hallowed weapon of the hunger strike against internment and prison rules. One of these was Sean McCaughey, from Auchnacloy in County Tyrone, who in 1941 defied the authorities at Portlaoise prison, where the rule was that only prison clothes could be worn. McCaughey spent four and a half years wearing only his cell blanket and ultimately went on a hunger strike which ended with his death in May, 1946. One man who saw him soon afterwards recalled that: 'his tongue had shrunk to the size of a threepenny piece.' His coffin was paraded through Dublin in front of large crowds prior to his burial in Belfast's Milltown Cemetery.

The years of the 'emergency' drew the IRA into military actions beyond its resources and deepened political and personal divisions within it. It was hard hit too, by coercive measures applied on both sides of the Irish border and in Britain and there was little its leaders could claim to have achieved as the war in Europe ended. Regrouping and new thinking were needed and a real rebirth of the IRA only came in response to events in Northern Ireland twenty five years later. Yet the cause remained and could reach out to those who, with the poet W B Yeats, could say:

> 'Out of Ireland have we come
> Great hatred, little room
> Maimed us at the start.
> I carry from my Mother's womb
> A fanatic heart.'

Identity Card photographs of Herman Goertz, a key German Agent, captured in Ireland in November 1941. He was interned at the Curragh camp and released on parole on 10 September 1946. Goertz committed suicide at the Aliens registration Office in Dublin Castle the following year.

CHAPTER 4

NORTHERN IRELAND
AT WAR

When Britain declared war on Germany on 3 September 1939, Viscount Craigavon, formerly Sir James Craig, had been Prime Minister of Northern Ireland since its creation by the Government of Ireland Act almost twenty years before. In the previous year he had led his Ulster Unionist party to a fifth successive victory in elections to the province's Parliament, which had met, since 1932, in the impressive if perhaps neo-Colonial Stormont building completed that year.

Elections were not difficult for Unionists to win in a mini-state constructed in 1920 to give them a permanent and built-in majority at elections whether to their own devolved Parliament or to Westminster. Craigavon, a Daily Express article had observed in 1938, was a politician who 'can win an election without even leaving his fireside.' Others were of the opinion that he took a minimalist view of his Prime Ministerial duties. He was sixty seven years old when war came and, as his own and his wife's health declined, spent increasing periods cruising in the Mediterranean in winter. If his position became vacant, some Belfast humorists put it, 'only good sailors need apply.'

Nonetheless, Craigavon had always been tenacious in his defence of Northern Ireland's constitutional rights and was revered by the Protestant community as a living symbol and dependable champion of their right to live apart from Eire and under the British crown. As Prime Minister he was never blindly hostile to the Irish state but was always a tough negotiator with it, as indeed he also was with London at any point where Northern Ireland's special status seemed to be at risk. The six county state's acute social problems were not one of his priorities. In the two years before the Stormont buildings were completed, he concerned himself intimately with their design and construction, yet over this period mass unemployment and hunger drove both Catholic and Protestant working class communities to desperation.

In 1932, when starvation rates of

LEFT: Belfast city children were evacuated into safer country areas for the duration of the Blitz.

ABOVE: Inspection of troops.

ABOVE: The Presentation of Shamrocks. This tradition dates back to 1900. Left to Right: Bandmaster Brooks, Mrs Burke-Murphy, Lt Col Burke-Murphy. 30th Battalion Royal Irish Fusiliers, St Patrick's Day 1943 at Mourne Park, Kilkeel, Co Down.

LEFT: C.O. of the Royal Irish Fusiliers presenting Shamrock, 17 March 1941 at the 25th Infantry Training Centre, Ballykinlar.

pay for 'outdoor relief' labour for the unemployed brought protest marches on to the streets of West Belfast, Craigavon and his ministers endorsed heavy-handed intervention by the Royal Ulster Constabulary which resulted in two people being shot dead. Three years later, when the July parade season led to vicious sectarian riots on the North side of the city, he again relied on police action, though this time the RUC had to be supported by British troops. This was a community divided by the fault lines both of class and religious difference yet Craigavon read no implications into a speech he once made as Prime Minister in which he famously described Stormont as 'a Protestant Parliament for a Protestant people'.

Whether Craigavon's ageing Cabinet would be equal to the tasks war would bring worried the head of the Stormont civil service, Sir Wilfrid Spender. On 2 August he committed to paper his private doubts about them, as well as his anxiety about the Prime Minister's worsening health. When war was declared, the Northern Ireland Parliament was recalled by the Governor-General from its summer recess and Craigavon addressed an expectant Commons chamber pledging renewed loyalty to the Crown and full support for Britain's war effort.

Two days later, in conformity with London policy, national registration of Northern Ireland's entire population was announced from Stormont as a necessary basis for likely wartime rationing and commodity controls. To allay suspicions that this might be a prelude to conscription in the province Craigavon had to explain the operation to Parliament on 19 September, stressing it had no relationship to the Military Training Act which did not apply to Northern Ireland. Craigavon had in fact unsuccessfully urged on the Chamberlain government in April 1939 the case for conscription being applied to the province and he resented London's preoccupation with what was assumed would be the hostile reaction of the nationalist community.

He had, however, to be less outspoken in his anger than his Unionist colleague Sir Basil Brooke. He publicly attributed Chamberlain's inaction on the issue to the existence in their midst 'of a minority who, whilst prepared to share in the benefits of Empire, were either afraid or too despicable to take a hand in the defence of the country which defended them and were prepared to go to any length to prevent loyal and brave men from doing their duty.'

Such men were certainly there, yet, without any call-up there was no dramatic rush to the colours in Northern Ireland in

1939. There was never going to be within a minority community who accorded scant legitimacy to what they saw as a British-imposed partitionist state. Neither was there any great rush to volunteer from within the Unionist population of military age, something which greatly troubled both Stormont ministers and Unionist leaders.

This anxiety is echoed in the official history of Northern Ireland at war specially commissioned by the Unionist government well ahead of victory in Europe. The slaughter on the Somme and the bitter years on the dole which followed for many survivors of it, cast a long shadow over even the streets of a Loyalist heartland like the Shankill in West Belfast. Yet only a couple of miles away, on the south side of the city, the response in the then strongly Unionist Queen's University was not initially conspicuous. Its Vice-Chancellor, Sir David Lindsay Keir, felt compelled to send out a letter in his own name to all staff and undergraduates, putting it to them that academic study was not a reason for deferring enlistment.

When the Grand Orange Lodge of Ireland announced in the summer of 1940 that all its scheduled parades to commemorate the Protestant victory at the Boyne in 1690, were being cancelled, cynics responded with the view that this would at least conceal the large numbers of able-bodied Orangemen of military age who were showing their loyalty by remaining loyally at home. In traditionally Protestant industries like shipbuilding and engineering there was, after 1939, the guarantee of secure wartime pay in reserved occupations. There was also enlarged wartime recruitment to the RUC and its B-Special reserve force. Some of them of course saw their role as being as much to defeat the IRA as to defeat Hitler.

One Belfast Protestant who did enlist in 1940 in the RAF and who saw much active service as an aircrew member, was Sam McAughtry. He later wrote a fine memoir of his time with the RAF, called *McAughtry's War*. In it he recalled returning after the war to his home in North Belfast and going into a local pub where he was at once recognised by an off-duty RUC officer. The returned hero was bought a pint then slipped an application form for joining the B-Special reserve, with the words from the RUC man: 'That's in case a real war starts.'

What created acute unrest in Unionist minds was the thought that the number enlisting from their community might be matched or surpassed by the response from across the border or even from within the nationalist population in Northern Ireland. There was no real danger of the latter happening. Sectarian and

ABOVE: Military Ball, Newcastle. The Royal Irish Fusiliers regimental band at a military ball in the Slieve Donard Hotel on 16 June 1944. The 25th Infantry Training Centre was at nearby Ballykinlar. The Union Jack and Stars and Stripes have photographs of Prime Minister Winston Churchill, Chiang Kai-Shek, Joesph Stalin and President Roosevelt.

political divisions were too deep but among Northern Catholics who did join up, a variety of factors influenced them, such as a family tradition of military service or guilt at the thought of not joining an anti-Fascist 'people's war'. Their bravery on many fronts is well documented as is their good relations with Protestant comrades in arms. This is perhaps best exemplified after the liberation of Rome when pipers and drummers of the 38th Irish Brigade played for the Pope in St Peter's Square. Most of them were from Ulster regiments and Orangemen happily paraded alongside Catholics.

Pressure within the minority community not to enlist or to give any form of support to the British war effort could be as strong as it was narrow-minded and insular. This is nowhere better captured than in Brian Moore's novel *The Emperor of Ice Cream*. The central character, a Catholic Belfast teenager, mystifies and indeed shocks his extended family by joining the Air Raid Precaution Service, the ARP. His father, soon to change his tune after the carnage of the April 1941 Belfast blitz, declares that 'when it comes to grinding down minorities, the German jackboot isn't half as hard as John Bull.'

This does not deter the boy from his decision to join the civil defence services at a time when IRA graffiti on walls and gables in Catholic areas were denouncing it.

In the course of his time with the ARP, he meets two friends from his old school who have gone a step further and been accepted by the RAF for aircrew training. One of them has his own personal reasons: 'I hear the women over in England are starved of men and hot as coals. If I die, at least it won't be in trying to get between the thighs of some cold Irish virgin. That uniform is going to liberate me.'

The issue of conscription would not go away and as the war intensified the case for extending it to Northern Ireland was inevitably reopened. Early in 1941 Churchill's Minister of Labour, Ernest Bevin, was advised that 50,000 men could be quickly raised by a call-up in Northern Ireland. Support for this revived within the Stormont Cabinet. Some ministers felt that the horror of the Belfast blitz, which had killed Catholics and Protestants indiscriminately, would make conscription in some form more acceptable. Others clearly saw it as a useful instrument with which to control a population resentful over Belfast's grossly inadequate protection from air attack and taking part increasingly in strikes in vital war industries.

In late May 1941, John Andrews, who had replaced Craigavon as Prime Minister the previous November, went to London with four of his ministers to put an agreed case for conscription to Bevin and

ABOVE: A tank exercise, April 1941. Light tanks of a yeomanry unit out on an exercise in Northern Ireland.

the Home Secretary, Herbert Morrison. Their intentions were already known and were condemned from predictable quarters.

Cardinal Joseph MacRory, Archbishop of Armagh and Primate of All Ireland, declared that 'Ireland was an ancient land, made one by God, but partitioned by a foreign power, against the vehement protests of its people. Conscription would now seek to compel those who writhe under this grievous wrong to fight on the side of its perpetrators.' The Cardinal was fervently anti-British, if not actually pro-German, but his voice was joined by that of the Northern Ireland Labour Party, always since its formation in 1924 divided over what its stance on partition and the national question should be. It was led by a Protestant, Harry Midgley, who had fought at the Somme in 1916 but had already opposed conscription in the opening weeks of the war.

De Valera's own condemnation was passed on to Churchill by John Dulanty, Eire's High Commissioner in London. This provoked an angry diatribe by the Prime Minister, although he did agree to pass the Taoiseach's views to the Cabinet. Possibly the key role was that of the RUC's Inspector-General, as the force's senior officer was then called. He was Lieutenant-Colonel Charles Wickham, who went to London with the Stormont ministers. In his

assessment of the issue he stressed the IRA's ability to exploit it in nationalist areas and also the need, however difficult it might be, to apply conscription fairly to both communities. Good evidence suggests that Protestant Northern Ireland was not as enthusiastic for it as its leadership.

On 27 May 1941 the British government announced that there would be no conscription in Northern Ireland. Nonetheless some Unionists clung to the possibility of London having a change of mind, if only to apply conscription as a way of counteracting the anticipated loss of jobs at the war's end when military contracts for the province's industries began to dry up. This was of course a wholly unrealistic expectation. No London government was going to use a regional call-up simply for economic reasons and at a point when no real risk to the conscripts would be involved.

Forms of military service which fell well short of conscription for Northern Ireland were also fraught with difficulties which mirrored its sectarian divisions. On 28 May 1940, following the huge success of recruitment to Britain's Local Defence Volunteers, better known as the Home Guard, the Stormont government announced plans to raise a similar force. The reality of Eire's neutrality, German victories in the West and the strategic

TOP: 30th Battalion Royal Irish Fusiliers, St Patrick's Day 1943 at Mourne Park, Kileel, Co Down. Lt Col Burke-Murphy taking the salute.

LEFT: Field Marshal Gort inspecting a guard of the battalion, July 1941, at the 25th Infantry Training Centre Ballykinlar. First published in the Royal Irish Fusiliers regimental gazette.

importance of Northern Ireland, made its defence an obvious priority. All this, however was overshadowed by Lord Craigavon's announcement that the Home Guard would be raised as a branch of the RUC's special reserve force.

His reason for this was to prevent republican infiltration of the new defence force. It, he made clear, would be under the authority of the RUC's Inspector-General, not as in Britain, under military command. As a result, the few Catholics who joined up mostly left fairly quickly because of their long aversion to the B-Special men who formed the Home Guard's nucleus. Strong criticism of the Stormont government's handling of the issue drew in ministers in London, with the Home Office and War Office disagreeing over the case for overruling Stormont. In the end Churchill declined to act. Moya Woodside, a Belfast doctor's wife whose diaries compiled for Mass Observation are a valuable source on wartime Northern Ireland, wrote that the new Home Guard had simply been turned into 'a sectarian body'. This at least was never allowed to happen in units of the British forces in which volunteers from Northern Ireland's two communities served side by side on many war fronts.

Craigavon's government had once again revealed its fear of the republican enemy within the gate and the IRA had of course already launched a bombing campaign in Britain.

Its fears went beyond the IRA's military potential, limited as it proved to be, to the bitter issue of how far Churchill might be ready to compromise with Eire over partition in order to bring it into the war as an ally, or simply to secure renewed access to the Treaty ports. Events coinciding with Hitler's invasion of the west and the fall of France proved these fears justified.

'The European position is so serious,' wrote Sir Wilfred Spender in May 1940, 'that there is no knowing what sacrifices may be necessary for Northern Ireland to make.' British intelligence was already alert to the IRA's German contacts and in Cabinet on 12 June, Chamberlain urged the case for talks with both the Stormont government and de Valera on defence co-operation. These took place and have been described in an earlier chapter. They involved an end to partition becoming a basis for British access to the Treaty ports, proof of the mounting sense of crisis in London.

Craigavon, once informed of the British offer, reacted with incandescent rage. 'To such treachery to Loyal Ulster I will never be a party', he wrote to Chamberlain. He, authorised by Churchill, gave the Stormont leader little comfort with his reply: 'You can be assured that you will have every opportunity of making your views known before any decision affecting Ulster is taken. Meanwhile, please remember the serious nature of the situation, which requires that every effort be made to meet it.'

Craigavon's response did not echo the view of all his colleagues. Sir Basil Brooke, Agriculture Minister, and John McDermott, the Security Minister, were of the opinion that the need to defeat Hitler was more important than the union and that some change in Northern Ireland's constitutional position might be an unavoidable price to pay for bringing Eire into the war as an ally of Britain. A possible Unionist schism was averted by de Valera's rejection of the British offer since he saw no need to trade off Irish neutrality for promises from a government whose days would be numbered if Britain's military situation got any worse.

By December 1941, Ulster Unionism had a new leader and the province a new Prime Minister. John Andrews was elected by Stormont Unionist MPs after Craigavon's death in November 1940, and had been Finance Minister prior to his appointment. He was of Scottish planter stock from Comber in County Down, with a solid record of success in the linen business and a secure base in both Unionism and the Orange Order. He had not long to wait for a major crisis which would brutally expose the shortcomings of Unionist rule.

From the night of 7 April 1941 and then at intervals until 8 May, Belfast suffered a series of air attacks which were among the heaviest unleashed by the Luftwaffe on the British Isles. The loss of life and destruction which resulted was accentuated by the city's inadequate defences and its shortage of deep shelter provision. The latter, coupled with the density of poor standard housing in working class localities, caused a terrible death roll among Belfast's poorest, both Catholic and Protestant.

The Redemptorist Order's beautiful monastery church off Clonard Street in West Belfast, which in 1969 would be at the epicentre of sectarian violence because of its closeness to Loyalist areas, opened its deep cellars to Protestants fleeing for sanctuary as their streets burned in April 1941. Thousands more fled the city altogether. Moya Woodside described roads leading out of the city choked with vehicles and people on foot as panic spread at the prospect of renewed attacks.

For the first time, householders in the suburbs and nearby country areas who offered refuge to the survivors of the blitz, encountered the poverty of so many of Belfast's population and were deeply

RIGHT: J.M. Andrews, Prime minister of Northern Ireland, 1940-43. Sir Basil Brooke replaced Andrews for the remainder of the war.

ABOVE: A Tank Exercise. A British official War Office photograph of light tanks of a yeomanry unit out an exercise in Northern Ireland. One of the crew of a light tank is shown making an adjustment, April,1941.

LEFT: Soldiers of the Royal Irish Fusiliers resting on a route march top, and getting dressed, below. They were based at the 25th Infantry Training Centre at Ballykinlar, dated January 1940.

BELOW: Officer's and NCO's of H Company Royal Irish Fusiliers at 25th Infantry Training Centre, Ballykinlar, January 1944.

ABOVE: Nurses at work in Belfast.
OVERLEAF: Belfast after a raid.

shocked and in some cases repelled by it. Back in the city, the emergency and rescue services, famously helped by the Dublin fire brigade, fought a losing battle against the aftermath of the German attacks. The worst night was that of 15-16 April, but in total more than 1,100 people died and 100,000 were made temporarily homeless.

Dr Brian Barton has written a graphic account of events, drawing upon survivors' recollections and quoting witnesses of awful scenes as the Falls Road and Peter's Hill swimming baths were emptied of water to create temporary mortuaries.

St George's Market was also used for this purpose and one nurse who had served on the Western Front over twenty years before, was appalled by what she saw there. 'Death here,' she later wrote, 'was grotesque, repulsive, horrible. No attendant nurse had soothed the last moments of these victims, no gentle, reverent hand had closed their eyes or crossed their hands. With tangled hair, staring eyes, clutching hands, contorted limbs, their grey-green faces covered with dust, they lay, bundled into the coffins, half-shrouded in rugs or blankets, or an occasional sheet, still wearing their dirty, torn, twisted garments.

Death should be dignified, peaceful; Hitler had made even death grotesque.'

The Stormont government had the power to provide Belfast with a network of deep shelter provision but had used it sparingly. It had also allowed the emergency services to remain undermanned, though within the nationalist community there was active hostility to recruitment by them. Andrews and his ministers faltered in their answers to questions about these issues and were slow to respond to the scale of the housing crisis created by the blitz.

They suffered politically as a result. In a December 1941 Stormont by-election, they lost the previously safe Willowfield seat in Belfast to Harry Midgley of the Northern Ireland Labour Party. His support of the union and the border was not in doubt and he wore his First World war medals during a campaign in which he poured scorn on Unionist misrule and called for urgent action to tackle social problems which the war was accentuating.

A new crisis confronted Andrews and his colleagues when in March 1942 the IRA's Northern Command decided to renew operations against the Crown forces. Arrests and internment of activists in response to the September 1939 bombing

The first black GI's created quite a stir in Northern Ireland. All American forces were considered, along with the other Allies, a possible IRA target. Nationalist areas of Belfast were declared off-limits to GIs.

Tom Williams.
The first and last IRA man to be executed by the
Northern Irish state.

campaign had seriously weakened the organisation on both sides of the border but the Belfast leadership was committed to another show of strength, even though the resources for this were limited. The authorities had to take the threat seriously as the growing number of British troops as well as American forces were a possible IRA target.

In the event, they largely escaped attack though nationalist areas of Belfast were declared off-limits to GIs, whose presence on Irish soil de Valera had described as an affront. Easily the most famous IRA operation was mounted by the organisation's C Company in the Clonard area of West Belfast in early April 1942. This was intended as a diversion to draw the RUC away from Milltown cemetery, where an illegal commemoration of the 1916 Easter rising was planned.

A six-man IRA unit ambushed a police patrol in Kashmir Street and then retreated to a nearby house where they exchanged further fire with the RUC, killing a Catholic constable, Paddy Murphy. Six IRA men were convicted of responsibility for his death, among them Joe Cahill, who in the 1970s became Provisional IRA Chief of Staff. In response to a powerful campaign across nationalist Ireland, all but one of the convicted men were reprieved, on 30 August 1942.

Tom Williams, a nineteen year old lieutenant in C Company of his local IRA unit, was chosen for execution and sentence was carried out two days later in Crumlin Road prison. Appeals to London, Washington and the Vatican for intervention failed to save him and women from the republican movement prayed on their knees for him outside the prison as the moment for his hanging approached. As it did, they were taunted by Loyalists from nearby Protestant areas, who sought to drown out their prayers with Orange songs.

Williams, the first and last IRA man to be executed by the Northern Irish state, attained iconic status in death. What was claimed to be his final message from the death cell – 'Thank all for the efforts to save me. I am quite resigned, if it is God's Holy Will and if it is done for Ireland' – was widely circulated and songs and ballads perpetuated his memory. Paddy Devlin, interned as a teenager soon afterwards for suspected IRA membership, recalled years later in his memoirs how as a boy he had happily played football with both Williams and the murdered RUC man's son, a reminder of the close-knit community that was West Belfast and still is.

For nearly sixty years, Tom Williams' remains lay in an unmarked grave in the grounds of Crumlin Road prison. It took years of demands from the republican

Organised by Belfast
National Graves Association

Tom Williams

RE-INTERMENT
COMMEMORATION

Sun 23 Jan 2000

ASSEMBLE:
12.30pm Clonard Street

movement and the National Graves Association to have them exhumed and re-interred in Milltown. A combination of the closure of the grim old prison and the advent of the peace process assisted this outcome. On Sunday 23 January 2000, much of West Belfast came to a standstill for a macabre piece of republican street theatre as a coffin containing the remains of Tom Williams was paraded up the Falls Road for burial. All the Sinn Fein leadership attended, taking turns to carry the coffin but at the request of surviving relatives, Williams was laid to rest beside members of his family, not in the cemetery's republican plot where many IRA volunteers killed much more recently are buried.

The hanging inevitably drove up the level of tension in republican areas and along the border where IRA raiding columns from Eire launched attacks. There were gun battles in Belfast and on 5 September, a sixteen year old IRA volunteer, Gerry Adams, later to be the father of a much more famous son, was shot and wounded in an attack on the RUC no distance from where Tom Williams had been arrested four months earlier. By the time he was brought to trial in October 1942, two of his brothers had been interned and he himself was convicted on the lesser charge of illegal possession of ammunition. His police file described him as 'honest, sober, industrious and generally of good character – except for the fact that he was known to associate with members of the IRA.'

His sentencing, to an eight year term, only half of which he served, came at a point when the IRA's new campaign was losing momentum. There were dramatic episodes like its Chief of Staff, Hugh McAteer, escaping with two other prisoners from Crumlin Road jail in January 1943. Over the eight months in which he was at liberty before being recaptured, McAteer found it hard to re-activate the campaign. Too many key volunteers were either interned or in prison. Most of them, like their comrades south of the border, sat out the rest of the war in prison cells or workshops. For those, like Paddy Devlin, who used their time to read, study and argue politics with other prisoners, it was a formative time.

He wrote later of how prisoners' and internees' morale declined as IRA operations dwindled to little of any significance but also of some shifts in political attitudes: 'Discussions on the rights and wrongs of the war were well to the fore. It was surprising to hear words of praise for Britain's part in fighting the Fascist forces of Hitler and Mussolini. I began to understand better the reasons for the war, and to recognise that there were many admirable

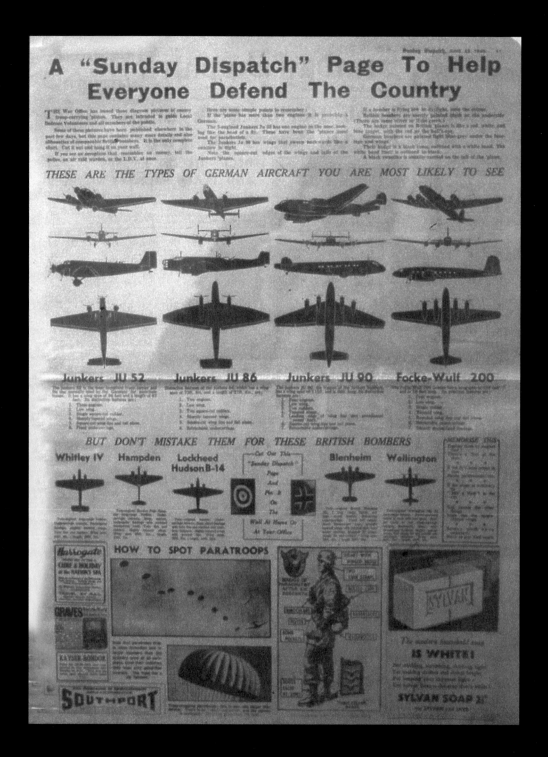

ABOVE: A Newspaper guide to German bombers.

values in the British people. It was as if I emerged from a tunnel of darkness.'

The IRA's failure was not enough to raise the flagging fortunes of the Andrews government. Long standing rumours of corruption and patronage on the Unionist-run Belfast City Corporation produced only an indecisive response from the government. It was only strong Opposition pressure that made Andrews accept, in June 1942, legislation to suspend the corporation and appoint three administrators in its place. Neither did the government's handling of industrial unrest do much for its credibility

The official History of Northern Ireland at War, published in 1956, gives little space to this, yet constant reports reached both Stormont and Whitehall departments of poor workplace morale, inept management, absenteeism and recurrent strikes. Churchill himself expressed his shock at a dispute over Sunday shifts in the engineering industry which by late September 1942 brought over 10,000 workers out on strike in vital aircraft production factories in Belfast.

Andrews had no initiatives to offer in response to these problems and found himself under increasing attack over the growing scandal of the condition of Belfast's blitz evacuees and their grossly inadequate accommodation. He showed

himself to be adrift too in the debate within Northern Ireland on the November 1942 Beveridge Report on postwar welfare policy. Yet early the next year Andrews surprised everyone by the determination with which he clung to his position. As late as 16 April, the Ulster Unionist Council's 750 delegates affirmed by acclamation their support for him. Twelve days later however, when the Unionist Party's Stormont MPs met at their Belfast office, it became clear that as many as six ministers would leave the Cabinet if Andrews continued and he resigned without a formal note being taken.

The new Prime Minister, Sir Basil Brooke, later to become Viscount Brookeborough, was a classic representative of the 'big house' Unionist tradition. He owned a large estate in County Fermanagh and had served with distinction in the army. After leaving it at the end of the First World War he played an uncompromising role in the creation and initial defence of the Unionist state and some of his public remarks, apparently justifying employment practices which favoured Protestants did little to endear him to the minority community. He was, however, an effective minister, first of Agriculture, then from 1940 to 1943, of Commerce, in the Andrews government and was committed to maximising Northern Ireland's contribution to a war in which two of his three sons were killed in action.

153

Brooke led Northern Ireland through the remainder of the war, a period which saw a significant improvement in both industrial relations and output. This went some way to justify his own, and Churchill's claims, for what the province had contributed to ultimate victory, even if its enlistment levels continued to fall short of what the Unionist government had hoped for. The Brooke government broke some new ground by appointing as its Minister of Public Security, Harry Midgley, who had founded a new Commonwealth Labour Party to press the case for postwar social justice and welfare policies within the Union.

Brooke was much more adept than his predecessor in consulting Ulster Unionist MPs at Stormont over policy and in 1944 he was able to carry them with him on increases in the state's funding of the maintained or Catholic school system and also the creation of a Housing Trust which could act independently of local councils. Many of these had a poor record, both in actual building and of religious discrimination in letting policy. These were significant moves but in the same year the Unionist government steered well clear of any action to assimilate the local council franchise, which permitted plural and property-based voting, to that used for Westminster and Stormont elections. This failure of Brooke's, which maintained in place a system that helped entrench local Unionist power even though it also denied votes to many working class Protestants, became a central demand twenty years later of the mainly Catholic Civil Rights campaign. This would do far more than the IRA and the war to de-stabilise Unionist rule.

It emerged intact from the war. There was no counterpart in Northern Ireland to Labour's landslide victory across the Irish Sea in July 1945. The Ulster Unionists held their ground securely in the Westminster poll and in the Stormont General Election the same month they won 33 out of the 50 available seats though the vote for the Northern Ireland Labour Party and other radical groupings grew substantially.

The mini-state which Brooke led was happy to bask in Churchill's praise for its wartime role yet it remained, in 1945, as divided a community as it had been six years earlier. Soldiers serving there often became very aware of this, whether British or American, though the latter of course also brought their own country's racial tensions with them.

Operations by the IRA, limited though these were in the province, and

LEFT: Surrendered German submarines at Lisakelly, Northern Ireland.

155

ABOVE: Queen Elizabeth (1900-2002) on a visit to Belfast.
RIGHT: A barrage balloon near an allotment.

TOP: The cenotaph outside City Hall, Belfast.
BELOW: Stained glass window from inside the Waring Street museum in Belfast devoted to the Second World War. A plaque outside states 'This hall is a perpetual reminder of the friendship between the people of Northern Ireland and the American Forces who served in the Province during the Second World War.'

pro-German sentiment within the organisation's ranks did nothing to reduce Loyalist suspicion of a minority population which could be accused of harbouring it. Within the Catholic church too, there had been at the very least an ambivalence towards Britain's cause which could be easily linked to Eire's neutrality.

Many Loyalists then, as they still do, took a simplistic view of this and the reasons for it. It was easy for them to identify the Catholic community with what was seen as de Valera's desertion of Britain in 1939. His ill-judged offer of condolences to the German legation in Dublin on Hitler's death was pressed into service to support their case, almost as often as the claim that Hitler's bombers reached Belfast, hardly a difficult target for them, with the aid of black-out violations from nationalist areas.

One man, a true hero, personified at the war's end Northern Ireland's continuing and bitter divisions. He was Leading seaman James Magennis, a Catholic from West Belfast who went to the school later attended by Gerry Adams. In 1945, as one of a midget submarine crew, he won the province's only Victoria Cross of the war for placing limpet mines on a Japanese cruiser in Singapore harbour. He did this despite the oxygen cylinder he carried starting to leak and his officer on the operation described him as the bravest man he had ever met.

On his return home, many of Belfast's Unionist councillors were reluctant to honour Magennis on the city's behalf while in the area where he had grown up he was castigated by many for having served with the British forces. Moving to the solidly Protestant east of the city did not solve his problems either, for he found himself suspect despite his war record.

His son later described the medal as being like a millstone round his father's neck. James Magennis eventually left Belfast for Bradford, where he died in 1986. Soon after the IRA's 1994 ceasefire, an ultimately successful campaign with support from both communities was launched to have a memorial erected to his memory. This was dedicated at a ceremony on the lawn outside Belfast City Hall on 9 October, 1999. The republican movement did not feel able to be represented, however. One of its Sinn Fein councillors declared that: 'The current political climate would not allow us to attend – he was a member of the British forces.'

LEFT: Auxillery fireman at work in Belfast.

RIGHT: Belfast after a raid.

TOP AND BELOW: Belfast prison Identification photographs of Gerry Adams senior, taken 30 December 1942 and 19 December 1946, respectively.

Appendix to the Calendar of Prisoners for Trial

at BELFAST CITY COMMISSION : 24.11.42.

(Young Offenders 16 to 21 years of age)

PREVENTION OF CRIME ACT, 1908, SECTION 1 (1).

As modified by Section 18 (*c*) *and amended by the Criminal Justice Administration Act*, 1914.

" Where a person is convicted on indictment of an offence for which he is liable to be sentenced to penal servitude or imprisonment, and it appears to the court—

" (a) that the person is not less than sixteen nor more than twenty-one years of age ; and

" (b) that, by reason of his criminal habits or tendencies, or association with persons of bad character, it is expedient that he should be subject to detention for such term and under such instruction and discipline as appears most conducive to his reformation and the repression of crime ;

it shall be lawful for the court, in lieu of passing a sentence of penal servitude or imprisonment, to pass a sentence of detention under penal discipline in a Borstal Institution for a term of not less than two years nor more than three years ;

" Provided that, before passing such a sentence; the court shall consider any report or representations which may be made to it by or on behalf of the General Prisons Board as to the suitability of the case for treatment in a Borstal Institution, and shall be satisfied that the character, state of health, and mental condition of the offender, and the other circumstances of the case, are such that the offender is likely to profit by such instruction and discipline as aforesaid."

| No. in Calendar. | 12. | THE KING *V.* | Gerald Adams. | 16–5/12 Years. |

Health GOOD, Physique GOOD, Mental Condition NORMAL, and Medically UNFIT for Borstal Treatment. Medical Report states :- Has 3 Gunshot wounds - 1. Rt. Groin, healed. 1. Lt. knee, healed, but movement restricted. 1. Lt. Hand, healed. Uses crutches.
He is charged with Attempt Murder of Constables James Lorimer and Robert Elkin at Belfast on 5.9.42. Also with Unlawful Possession of Firearms and Ammunition with Intent to Endanger Life, etc., and with Possession of Explosive Substances for an Unlawful Object, at the same time and place. This is believed to be the first occasion of his being charged with a criminal offence.
The Police report that he has been honest, sober, industrious, and generally of GOOD character - except for the fact that he was known to associate with members of the I.R.A. - prior to being charged with this offence.
The Police also further report the character of his relatives, friends and Associates as GOOD, but known to have I.R.A. connections.(2 brothers interned His mother is willing to receive and assist him if acquitted, or after he has served such sentence as may be imposed by the Court.

The Governor of the Prison, or his representative in Court, can give more detailed information if required.

ABOVE: Appendix from prosecution report on Gerry Adams senior.

LEFT: Recruitment poster fror the Ulster Home Guard.
ABOVE: A Belfast Soldier of the Ulster Home Guard.

ABOVE AND LEFT: Women working in an ARP (Air Raid Precaution) Operations Room. Voluntary organisations such as the ARP and the Women's Voluntary Service, played important roles in Belfast's defence. However great damage was done to business and industry and civilian causualties were high. 180 German bombers took part in attack from midnight until 4a.m. Easter Tuesday, 1941. Over 900 people were killed that night. During World War II probably no other city within the United Kingdom, except London, lost so many of its citizens on a single night's raid.

ABOVE: York Street, near St Anne's Cathedral, Belfast after a bombing raid.

Issued by the Ministry of Information *in co-operation with the War Office and the Ministry of Home Security.*

If the
INVADER
comes

WHAT TO DO — AND HOW TO DO IT

THE Germans threaten to invade Great Britain. If they do so they will be driven out by our Navy, our Army and our Air Force. Yet the ordinary men and women of the civilian population will also have their part to play. Hitler's invasions of Poland, Holland and Belgium were greatly helped by the fact that the civilian population was taken by surprise. They did not know what to do when the moment came. *You must not be taken by surprise.* This leaflet tells you what general line you should take. More detailed instructions will be given you when the danger comes nearer. Meanwhile, read these instructions carefully and be prepared to carry them out.

I

When Holland and Belgium were invaded, the civilian population fled from their homes. They crowded on the roads, in cars, in carts, on bicycles and on foot, and so helped the enemy by preventing their own armies from advancing against the invaders. You must not allow that to happen here. Your first rule, therefore, is :—

(1) IF THE GERMANS COME, BY PARACHUTE, AEROPLANE OR SHIP, YOU MUST REMAIN WHERE YOU ARE. THE ORDER IS " STAY PUT ".

If the Commander in Chief decides that the place where you live must be evacuated, he will tell you when and how to leave. Until you receive such orders you must remain where you are. If you run away, you will be exposed to far greater danger because you will be machine-gunned from the air as were civilians in Holland and Belgium, and you will also block the roads by which our own armies will advance to turn the Germans out.

II

There is another method which the Germans adopt in their invasion. They make use of the civilian population in order to create confusion and panic. They spread false rumours and issue false instructions. In order to prevent this, you should obey the second rule, which is as follows :—

(2) DO NOT BELIEVE RUMOURS AND DO NOT SPREAD THEM. WHEN YOU RECEIVE AN ORDER, MAKE QUITE SURE THAT IT IS A TRUE ORDER AND NOT A FAKED ORDER. MOST OF YOU KNOW YOUR POLICEMEN AND YOUR A.R.P. WARDENS BY SIGHT, YOU CAN TRUST THEM. IF YOU KEEP YOUR HEADS, YOU CAN ALSO TELL WHETHER A MILITARY OFFICER IS REALLY BRITISH OR ONLY PRETENDING TO BE SO. IF IN DOUBT ASK THE POLICE-MAN OR THE A.R.P. WARDEN. USE YOUR COMMON SENSE.

III

The Army, the Air Force and the Local Defence Volunteers cannot be everywhere at once. The ordinary man and woman must be on the watch. If you see anything suspicious, do not rush round telling your neighbours all about it. Go at once to the nearest policeman, police-station, or military officer and tell them exactly what you saw. Train yourself to notice the exact time and place where you saw anything suspicious, and try to give exact information. Try to check your facts. The sort of report which a military or police officer wants from you is something like this :—

> "At 5.30 p.m. to-night I saw twenty cyclists come into Little Squashborough from the direction of Great Mudtown. They carried some sort of automatic rifle or gun. I did not see anything like artillery. They were in grey uniforms."

Be calm, quick and exact. The third rule, therefore, is as follows :—

(3) KEEP WATCH. IF YOU SEE ANYTHING SUSPICIOUS, NOTE IT CAREFULLY AND GO AT ONCE TO THE NEAREST POLICE OFFICER OR STATION, OR TO THE NEAREST MILITARY OFFICER. DO NOT RUSH ABOUT SPREADING VAGUE RUMOURS. GO QUICKLY TO THE NEAREST AUTHORITY AND GIVE HIM THE FACTS.

IV

Remember that if parachutists come down near your home, they will not be feeling at all brave. They will not know where they are, they will have no food, they will not know where their companions are. They will want you to give them food, means of transport and maps. They will want you to tell them where they have landed, where their comrades are, and where our own soldiers are. The fourth rule, therefore, is as follows :—

(4) DO NOT GIVE ANY GERMAN ANYTHING. DO NOT TELL HIM ANYTHING. HIDE YOUR FOOD AND YOUR BICYCLES. HIDE YOUR MAPS. SEE THAT THE ENEMY GETS NO PETROL. IF YOU HAVE A CAR OR MOTOR BICYCLE, PUT IT OUT OF ACTION WHEN NOT IN USE. IT IS NOT ENOUGH TO REMOVE THE IGNITION KEY; YOU MUST MAKE IT USELESS TO ANYONE EXCEPT YOURSELF.

IF YOU ARE A GARAGE PROPRIETOR, YOU MUST WORK OUT A PLAN TO PROTECT YOUR STOCK OF PETROL AND YOUR CUSTOMERS' CARS. REMEMBER THAT TRANSPORT AND PETROL WILL BE THE INVADER'S MAIN DIFFICULTIES. MAKE SURE THAT NO INVADER WILL BE ABLE TO GET HOLD OF YOUR CARS, PETROL, MAPS OR BICYCLES.

V

You may be asked by Army and Air Force officers to help in many ways. For instance, the time may come when you will receive orders to block roads or streets in order to prevent the enemy from advancing. Never block a road unless you are told which one you must block. Then you can help by felling trees, wiring them together or blocking the roads with cars. Here, therefore, is the fifth rule :—

(5) BE READY TO HELP THE MILITARY IN ANY WAY. BUT DO NOT BLOCK ROADS UNTIL ORDERED TO DO SO BY THE MILITARY OR L.D.V. AUTHORITIES.

VI

If you are in charge of a factory, store or other works, organise its defence at once. If you are a worker, make sure that you understand the system of defence that has been organised and know what part you have to play in it. Remember always that parachutists and fifth column men are powerless against any organised resistance. They can only succeed if they can create disorganisation. Make certain that no suspicious strangers enter your premises.

You must know in advance who is to take command, who is to be second in command, and how orders are to be transmitted. This chain of command must be built up and you will probably find that ex-officers or N.C.O.'s, who have been in emergencies before, are the best people to undertake such command. The sixth rule is therefore as follows :—

(6) IN FACTORIES AND SHOPS, ALL MANAGERS AND WORKMEN SHOULD ORGANISE SOME SYSTEM NOW BY WHICH A SUDDEN ATTACK CAN BE RESISTED.

VII

The six rules which you have now read give you a general idea of what to do in the event of invasion. More detailed instructions may, when the time comes, be given you by the Military and Police Authorities and by the Local Defence Volunteers; they will NOT be given over the wireless as that might convey information to the enemy. These instructions must be obeyed at once.

Remember always that the best defence of Great Britain is the courage of her men and women. Here is your seventh rule :—

(7) THINK BEFORE YOU ACT. BUT THINK ALWAYS OF YOUR COUNTRY BEFORE YOU THINK OF YOURSELF.

(52100) Wt. /   14,300,000 8/40 Hw.

ABOVE: Belfast after an attack. A Union Jack is visable amongst the rubble.

The Northern Whig

AND BELFAST POST

PEACE

Jap surrender ends War

"JAPAN HAS TO-DAY SURRENDERED. THE LAST OF OUR ENEMIES IS LAID LOW!"

Holiday to-day and to-morrow

King opens Victory Parliament to-day

ALL ALLIED OFFENSIVE ACTION CEASES

Premier thanks nation   *MacArthur to meet Japs*

Last day of Second World War

"PETAIN SENTENCED TO DEATH"

Sino-Russo friendship pact

How Britain heard the news

When Mother cannot feed Baby

HIROHITO TO TELL JAPS

"DEMOCRACY'S DAY"

CHAPTER 6

CONCLUSIONS

The Second World War, or the 'Emergency' as it is to this day called in the self-protectively euphemistic language of the Irish state, was a period of critical importance for it and for Eamon de Valera. His outwardly austere and unbending personality became inseparably linked to a policy of neutrality which he saw as being of a piece with everything he had tried to do in his period in office before 1939.

Over those 7 years, after all, in the face of bitter and highly personal attacks from his opponents, de Valera had shown just how far the boundaries to Irish sovereignty could be extended. He was aided in this by the British Statute of Westminster, enacted the year before he took power.

This immensely important piece of legislation recognised that British Dominions, to which category the Irish state still belonged under the 1921 treaty, were free to make laws regardless of their repugnance to British legislation. It also ended the application of British law to the Dominions except at their own request and it gave Dominion parliaments legislative power over their own nationals outside their own borders. The Crown, it also stated, was simply a symbol of the free association of the members of the British Commonwealth of Nations.

In the 1921 crisis preceding the Anglo-Irish treaty, de Valera had identified himself with the concept of an Irish state having 'external association' with the British Commonwealth in all matters of common concern and argued that such a state could accept the Crown as head of the Commonwealth without their being any need for an oath of allegiance to it. This was Document number 2, his alternative to the treaty actually signed. It would have allowed for British naval bases in Ireland for a five year period, subject to re-negotiation of their status after this time, and it involved de facto recognition of Northern Ireland's separate status.

Partly because de Valera excluded himself from the treaty talks, his Document did not arrive on the negotiating table and the Irish delegation in London signed up to an agreement which did put in place some potent symbols of British sovereignty over the new Free State, like the oath of allegiance and the office of Governor-General representing the Crown. Michael Collins justified accepting these terms as a tactical exercise which would give Ireland 'the freedom to win freedom' over time. This was a long game rejected by de Valera and the anti-Treaty IRA but in 1932, when he took office having entered the constitutional fold with many of his old comrades, the major symbols of British sovereignty remained.

Aided by the Statute of Westminster de Valera sought to remove or neutralise them. The Governor-General was ostracised in his public role and the oath of allegiance was abolished in 1932. De Valera linked these constitutional initiatives to the ending of Irish land annuities payable to Britain to help service its debt under the terms of the 1921 treaty. This he defended as a justifiable response to Britain's effective abandonment, in 1925, of the Boundary Commission set up under the treaty, supposedly to renew and adjust the 1920 borders.

Britain's answer was to apply tough import duties on Irish goods which had few other outlets. A bitter trade war, lasting six years, prompted a heightened nationalist rhetoric from Dublin, running in tandem with audacious moves to loosen and in effect end British sovereignty in the Irish state, as well as to assert an autonomous role for de Valera's government in the League of Nations.

Wartime neutrality must, therefore, be seen as the continuation of a successfully confrontational policy towards Britain. The skill with which de Valera played a less than strong hand after September 1939 won him an extended lease on political power and even those who had grown up to detest him and who felt deeply guilty about Irish neutrality, could find themselves identifying with the way he answered Churchill's ill-judged attack on their country in May 1945.

It was not, however, de Valera but his political opponents who, back in power in 1948, cut the final constitutional links with Britain. This was the work of John Costello, who had led the Fine Gael party to its first victory over de Valera in sixteen years. His announcement that Eire was becoming a full republic outside the Commonwealth was made in Ottawa on 7 September. A detailed plan of action had not been formulated in Cabinet and it may have been an impetuous move by the new Taoiseach to outflank his opponents by playing a republican trump card before they could.

But partition remained, underwritten by the Westminster Act of 1949, devised by a Labour government in response to Eire's decision to proclaim itself a republic. This set out in unequivocal terms that the border would remain for as long as a majority in Northern Ireland wanted it. This they clearly did, as a succession of subsequent elections in the Northern state would show. For de Valera, this reality was what he once called the 'rock on the road' to ultimate unification. Whether this rock would be blasted away by IRA guns and bombs or dismantled by the politics of compromise and reconciliations, would need another half century to decide.

Politically and personally, then, the 'Emergency' years can be seen as a triumph for de Valera. One of his biographers has entitled a chapter on his leadership in that period 'Finest Hour', a phrase more readily associated in Britain with Churchill and the spirit of 1940. Yet for a significant number of de Valera's compatriots the war years accentuated negative aspects of the Irish state and of Irish society. Censorship was a reality well before war and crisis arrived in 1939. The 'Emergency' was a pretext for tightening it and literary and cultural life felt the effects. 'The bleakness and meanness of material life in wartime', wrote the historian Oliver MacDonagh, 'were matched by emotional and intellectual impoverishment. In a society small, inward looking and self-absorbed, the general, compulsory and unheroic isolation reinforced all that was static or retrogressive in its composition.'

This view of Irish cultural life in the war years has for long been accepted and there were episodes which leant credibility to it, like the bile with which some of the Irish press responded to the death of James Joyce in another neutral state, Switzerland,

in 1941. The Irish Independent described him as 'having reviled the religion in which he had been brought up and fouled the nest which was his native city.'

Crass philistinism also manifested itself in the 1942 controversy over the decision by Dublin's Municipal Gallery of Modern Art to accept the gift of a painting by Georges Rouault. The Friends of the National Collection who had bought and then gifted to the Gallery Rouault's 'Christ and the Soldier' were accused in often vitriolic language, of sponsoring the blasphemous tendencies of French modernist art. Not all Catholic opinion took this view and the seminary at Maynooth defused the conflict by taking the canvas on loan to hang in its library. Years later, it was given its place in the Municipal Gallery.

One aspect of Eire's isolation during the 'Emergency' was that publishing outlets in Britain were virtually closed to Irish writers, as was the American market. Sean O'Faolain, the novelist and short story writer, reacted to this as a reminder of Irish literature's humiliating dependence on publishers outside the state's borders. When he accepted the editorship of The Bell, founded in 1940 as a magazine pledged to keep alive cultural debate and new writing, O'Faolain declared that 'The war has forced on us a cultural self-sufficiency more complete than the most fervent separatist could have imposed by law.'

ABOVE: Gerry Adams jr with his father Gerry Adams snr, 1950s.
By 1972 Gerry Adams emerged as a Provisional IRA leader, carrying on, as he saw it, the struggle his father had been part of thirty years earlier.

The Bell's first issue included contributions by Elizabeth Bowen, Patrick Kavanagh, Flann O'Brien, Frank O'Connor, Peadar O'Connell and Jack B. Yeats. Along with Dublin Opinion, the Bell became essential reading for literary Ireland on both sides of the border. Contributors and well-wishers often met in Dublin's Palace Bar where they sometimes had the wary company of plainclothes G2 and Garda Special Branch men anxious to monitor subversive conversation.

The political life of the Irish state was not transformed by the 'Emergency' years. There was no dramatic swing to Labour as in Britain, nor could there have been one, though the Irish Labour Party did well in the second wartime General Election of 1943, doubling its representation in the Dail to 17 seats. It was a short-lived triumph. Labour, under bitter attack from Sean McEntee, the Fianna Fail government's most strident conservative, saw its gains evaporate in the snap elections forced by the Taoiseach in May of the following year. Fianna Fail won a comfortable majority and de Valera was secure in power for another four years.

There was no break in the mould of Irish politics and no threat to de Valera's vision of the Ireland he was working for. Famously, in his Saint Patrick's Day broadcast to the people of Eire in 1943, he set this out: 'Acutely conscious as we all are of the misery and desolation in which the greater part of the world is plunged, let us turn aside for a moment to that ideal Ireland that we would have. That Ireland which we dreamed of would be the home of a people who valued material wealth only as the basis of right living, of a people satisfied with frugal comfort who devoted their leisure to the things of the spirit – a land whose countryside would be bright with cosy homesteads, whose fields and villages would be joyous with the sounds of industry, with the romping of sturdy children, the contests of athletic youths and the laughter of comely maidens, whose firesides would be forums for the wisdom of serene old age. It would, in a word, be the home of a people living the life that God desires that man should live.'

This comforting pastoral vision of Ireland left no real space for the asking of awkward questions or for social radicalism. Noel Browne, who returned home after spending the war years as both patient and doctor in English hospitals, found this when he entered politics as a member of Clann Na Phoblachta, a postwar grouping of left-leaning republicans formed in 1946. As Health Minister in the 1948 coalition government, he drew up proposals for free medical care for mothers and children under sixteen, only for Catholic bishops to denounce him for a sinister violation of church social teaching. Browne's party colleagues were quick to desert him as a brutal exercise of power by the church, and its compliant allies in the medical establishment, ended his ministerial career. Decades would pass before membership of what became the European Union began a slow transformation of the economic and social life of one of Europe's most conservative societies.

De Valera's inward-looking vision also excluded any real chance of a generous response to the Holocaust in German-occupied Europe. Blanket censorship protected Irish people from any real knowledge of it and state immigration law, dating back to the Aliens legislation of 1935, kept out Jews and other 'suspect' categories. A S Roche, secretary of the Department of Justice, felt able to write in 1945: 'The immigration of Jews is generally discouraged. They do not assimilate with our own people but remain a sort of colony of a world-wide Jewish community. This makes them a potential irritant in the body politic and has led to disastrous results from time to time in other countries.'

Eire did not discriminate against such Jews, a small number, who already had citizenship before 1939 and de Valera acted to stop the German and Italian legations disseminating anti-Semitic material. Nonetheless, there were crude expressions of prejudice against Jews in wartime Eire. Some of these were heard in the Dail itself and there were recorded cases of cinema audiences, especially in small towns and rural areas, being unwilling to believe newsreel film footage from Belsen and other concentration camps when it was screened in 1945.

In Kilkenny that year, one local newspaper claimed that film footage from Belsen was all propaganda faked by the British with the use of starving and emaciated Indian famine victims. For some Irish people, the belief in British imperialism as the real source of the world's evils was still deeply ingrained. As Dr Conor Cruise O'Brien put it in his memoirs in 1998: 'the idea that Nazism differed from all previously known imperialisms as Aids differs from the common cold was quite a new idea and unassimilable in our culture'. Some, perhaps many, Irish republicans would have accepted Irish unification as a gift from a victorious German Reich but there were 4,000 Jews in Eire in 1939 and it is well documented that Jews in what had been neutral states would have had no immunity from the murderous intentions of a German 'New Order' in Europe. How far the Irish state could have protected them, or would have wanted to, must remain problematic.

Mr Deasy declares to Stephen Dedalus in James Joyce's celebrated novel, *Ulysses,* that Ireland has the honour of being the only country which has never persecuted the Jews. When asked why, he says that this was because Ireland had never let them in. This was not wholly true but Jewish settlement remained small. Ten years

ABOVE: Churchill meets de Valera for the first time in the 1950s.

Spring 1945.
RIGHT: Concentration Camp
victims piled on carts as they were
discovered by the Allies after
liberating Buchenwald.
BELOW: American troops force the local
German population to confront the
horrors of concentration camps.

When newsreels of the Allies
liberating Europe, were first shown in
Ireland, some Irish cinema goers,
thought the images were faked by
British propaganda.

after the war's end, guilt over the Holocaust, if it even existed, was no impediment to an anti-Semitic campaign in Limerick, where cinemas were picketed and leafleted by zealots accusing them of corrupting audiences with the insidious products of a Jewish-controlled Hollywood. One of the activists was Father Denis Fahey, a member of the Holy Ghost Fathers, who recruited the willing services of Sean Sabhat or South, as he is better known. South became an IRA hero after his death in a raid across the Northern Ireland border in January 1957 and his feats were celebrated in a ballad which became popular in republican circles.

It took many years for official Ireland to render proper tribute to the Jewish victims of Nazi genocide. The way was cleared for this by the Provisional IRA's 1994 ceasefire in Northern Ireland. It occurred seven months after it, in April 1995, on the occasion of the re-opening and re-dedication of Dublin's Islandbridge memorial to Irishmen and women who lost their lives on Britain's side in the two world wars. The then Taoiseach, John Bruton, spoke eloquently of the Holocaust and made an unscripted reference to countries which 'closed their doors and their ports' to refugees from Nazi tyranny. His audience knew what he meant. With all political parties present, including Sinn Fein, it was the right moment for the Irish state and its people to be reminded that their neutrality

between 1939 and 1945, while perhaps a political necessity, had also involved some morally uncomfortable and less than heroic choices.

Half a century after Hitler's defeat, it was still a necessary reminder for a very different Irish state, long since a member of what had become the European Union and still benefiting disproportionately from it. There would have been no 'Celtic Tiger' economy, with the Gross National Product increasing over many years by an annual five per cent, without the European Union: but there would have been no European Union without the shared resolve of Britain and its allies to crush Nazi Germany.

In a new century, European good-will may not be an unlimited asset for Irish governments to draw upon. Many European Union states were angered by Dublin's reluctance to accept the military obligations involved in the proposed Partnership for Peace, an initiative which won the support of former Warsaw Pact states as well as that of NATO and of traditionally neutral countries.

It is a reluctance which de Valera would have understood and would certainly have been able to defend. Yet, at real cost to themselves, the Irish Republic's soldiers have at least played an honourable part in many dangerous United Nations peace-keeping operations around the world. De Valera would have understood that too, and applauded it.

The writer acknowledges for kind help and assistance:
Fianna Fáil,
Máirtín Breathnach of Ashville Media Group, Dublin, (35, 99, 101, 181)
Dr Seamus Healfearty of the Archives Department, University College Dublin, Belfield, (pages: 45, 46, 49, 52, 54)
Staff of the War Memorial Building, Waring Street, Belfast, (pages: 142, 144, 152, 156, 157, 160, 162, 166, 167, 169, 172, 174)
Helen Wood,
Belfast Telegraph, (pages: 22, 25, 126, 127)
British Pathe, (pages: 76, 102, 103, 106, 107)
The Embassy of the Federal Republic of Germany, in Dublin for the photograph of Dr Eduard Hempel, copyright Bundepresseamt (Federal Press and Information Office, Germany),
Japan Information and Cultural Centre, London,
Commandant Victor Laing of Military Archives, Dublin, (pages: 6, 36, 40, 56, 57, 65, 66, 68, 70, 74, 90, 124)
Liam Shannon of the National Graves Association, (pages: 110, 118, 148, 150)
Photograph of Gerry Adams, courtesy Deputy Keeper of the Records, the Public Records Office of Northern Ireland,
(also pages: 9, 18, 21, 26, 27, 29, 30, 31, 128, 137, 154, 164, 168, 170, 171)
Ballymurphy 25 years of Struggle, (page: 178)
US National Archives, (pages: 32, 105, 182)
Royal Irish Fusiliers Museum, Armagh, (pages: 129, 132, 134, 136, 140, 141)
Hulton-Getty collection, (pages: 93, 114, 115, 121)
Illustrated London News
John P. Duggan